# After Death . . . What?

# After Death . . . What?

by

William S. Deal

Beacon Hill Press of Kansas City
Kansas City, Missouri

Copyright, 1977
Beacon Hill Press of Kansas City

ISBN: 0-8341-0474-1

Printed in the
United States of America

# Contents

## *Preface*

This book is the result of many years of reading and serious reflection on one of the most profound subjects in the Bible.

The author here presents what have been the best arguments concerning the dead, their present abode, and final future state. Few quotations are made aside from the Bible itself and the meanings of several Hebrew and Greek original words. No matter how brilliant the mind or how wise the philosophical speculations, at the end of the argument they are merely that—simply speculations. No one has ever returned from that mysterious "great beyond," except Christ; He alone can tell us about its nature. The Bible and Jesus Christ are our only sources of true information about that state beyond this life. We have, therefore, drawn deeply from its perpetual fountain.

The author is most deeply indebted to his friend Karl Sabiers and his remarkable book, *Where Are the Dead?* This book is reported to have sold over 1 million copies in all editions during the past 20 years or more. The author has relied heavily on this source and wishes to express to Mr. Sabiers his deepest appreciation for the opportunity of doing so. I am also in heavy debt to Muncy, author of the most excellent book *Eternal Retribution,* now out of print. Another very good work long out of print is *Lost Forever,* by Townsend.

May God bless this work to the ministry of thousands.

—WILLIAM S. DEAL

# The Great Beyond and the Great Question

Centuries ago the patriarch Job cried in soul anguish, "Man dieth and wasteth away . . . and where is he?" In the next breath he asks, "If a man die, shall he live again?" Then in answer to his own questions, he shouts triumphantly, "I know that my redeemer liveth, and that he shall stand at the latter day upon the earth: and though after my skin worms destroy this body, yet in my flesh shall I see God: whom I shall see for myself . . . and not another" (Job 14:10, 14; 19:25-27).

Where are the dead? This question has rung out again and again down through the corridors of time. Where does man go after death? Does he become nonexistent, as atheists and scoffers assert? Or is he conscious in some other state of existence? Does real personality survive death? If so, in what form?

From times immemorial man has sought for the answers to these questions. The late Andrew Carnegie is reported to have offered $1 million to anyone who could prove to his satisfaction that there was life after death.

Apart from faith in God, man has carried in his bosom an aching void when he has sought the answer to this eternal question, Shall I live again when this life is over? Regardless of his professed atheistic or agnostic ideas, man yearns for life at its best and most—for life beyond this vale of sorrow and tears. The insatiable desire lies too deep in man's nature to be extinguished by mere doubt or personal rationalization.

In searching for the answer to Job's question, "If a man die, shall he live again?" let us turn to several sources.

1. *The answer from reason.* Reason alone, unaided by revelation, can never discover the full truth of the great beyond. It is as Alexander concluded in his book on *Moral Science* long ago: "Reason teaches us that there must be a God, but how to find Him, she teaches not." Building its answer upon all we know about human personality and its innate strivings and hungers, reason often concludes that there is a hereafter in which man will survive.

Job, who may have lived as early as the days of Abraham, and certainly no later than Solomon's time, expressed his profound conviction of faith in life hereafter.

Socrates, the father of Greek philosophy, believed in the immortality of the human soul. It is reported that he once lectured to a crowd about immortal life. It was so much superior to the current life that one poor heathen wanted to go immediately to the bosom of the gods and to dwell there eternally. He went immediately from Socrates' lecture and committed suicide.

2. *The answer from philosophy.* The goal of philosophy throughout the centuries has been to try and discover the primary purpose for which man exists and what are his highest goals and best good in life.

Philosophy, even aside from Holy Scripture, reckons that man's mentality is too superior to perish forever in the hour of death. His longings, insight into himself, understanding of morality, and his moral consciousness point to his survival in the great beyond.

Certainly the nature of man points to a being of far greater duration than a mere 70 years on this earth. By his connections with the past he brings with him a great store of knowledge and conviction. He develops a sense of moral awareness that does not belong to animals or to other life forms. Often this life is most unjust, and there is no reckoning which can rectify the unfairness. Life after death is required for mankind to make the proper adjustment to the demands of justice alone. This would argue, therefore, for the existence of man beyond his present era.

Everywhere, from the remotest past to the present hour, people have believed in the survival of the human spirit. In the most ancient lands, on the walls of the tombs and written into the rocks are signs that those who preceded us on earth believed in life after death for mankind. Archeology has done much to establish the fact of this general belief. One might say that the concept has been innate. From whence then came this belief, if not from the very nature of the human spirit? Even the Old Testament does not give a clear light on the nature of life after death. Thus this early yearning for survival did not come from direct revelation. It took the revelation of Christ to clarify the mists and give us the true light of what this eternal existence would be like.

3. *The answer from cosmology.* Scientists tell us that matter is perpetual, in that it is indestructible. It may be changed in form many ways and many times, such as water into steam, or wood reduced to ashes, but it can never be totally destroyed. Nothing is ever totally annihilated.

If this is true of matter, how much more is it bound to be true of the human spirit? There is no place where one can forever shed his personality or slip away from his spirit.

Man is a product of God from two sources—from nature and from the immortal Spirit of the Creator, who breathed into his nostrils, and man became a living soul. The body will die, but the soul man will forever take with him, wherever he may go after death.

4. *The answer from anthropology.* This branch of science seeks to understand man as a human being, whatever else he may be. He is a tripartite being. As understood by most theologians, he has a body, soul, and spirit. The fine distinction between spirit and soul will be made clearer further on. For now, let us think of man as a physical and spiritual being.

The body is a unit of flesh, blood, nerves, and bones; yet a total wholeness pervades it throughout. It is a unit, but not a unit that can survive death; all its qualities are reduced to dust by this harsh foe.

But the spiritual nature of man is something else. He is more than body—he is a rational, self-directing, intelligent, moral being—possessed of all the qualities necessary for eternal duration. Only the body is perishable. All man's other qualities are more durable than the stars. The mind never sleeps. The brain rests, but the mind is still active as is evidenced by dreams. Often these dreams are as clear as any waking thought—sometimes even more indelibly imprinted upon the memory.

Or again, take a look at the spiritual nature of man. Often old men manifest as keen an interest in life as when they were lads. The spiritual upsurge and longing for success or the outreach of faith are not limited by age. The spirit of man is forever youthful. Man's spirit may be as alive and alert at 100 as at 10. The spirit knows no age limits now, nor will it ever know any.

One can never think of soul and body as being the same. There is an inherent difference here as vast as the nature of man is different from that of animals. The spiritual nature of man rises above and beyond the mere physical as far as the stars are above the earth; and yet, as the earth and stars are all part of one universal system, so are soul and body part of one man. While the body is fastened to space by many anchors, the spirit may soar in mind and imagination thousands of miles away in a second's time. It knows no bounds of space. It is this boundless quality that will survive in death and live forever somewhere.

The whole perspective of mankind—his constitution, moral awareness, spiritual nature, psychological factors, and his long history as a believer in immortality—all argues in favor of his eternal existence.

Man has had this innate feeling of eternal survival wherever he has been found. Moffatt, the missionary, relates preaching to raw heathen in an African village. When he mentioned the resurrection of the body, the old chief stopped him. "The words of your mouth are sweet to me, Missionary," the chief said. "They are sweet like honey. But the words of a resurrection I cannot endure." Then raising his strong right arm, he declared, "This arm has killed thousands, and shall they rise again? Ah, no, I do not wish to hear about the dead rising again!"

Deep within his savage soul was a sense of justice, judgment, and the nature of survival beyond death. The words of resurrection penetrated his darkened spirit to arouse almost instant terror. The harmony of God's Word caught the harmony of his spiritual nature, and he became aware immediately of his soul's peril in its future. He did not attempt to deny that future, but fled in terror from its awful truth.

For the final answer we must turn now to the only Source from which it can come—*the answer from God's Word.*

# CHAPTER 2

# False Theories About the Dead

Far too little has been written by sound theologians from a scriptural viewpoint about the condition and activities of the dead. The cults have taken advantage of this in the past century to poison the minds of millions with their unorthodox literature. Far too many sincere Christians have been caught in these traps. They were simply poorly informed. But once they started down the pathway of cultism, it was hard to keep from going all the way.

One of the current cults dealing in this matter is Jehovah's Witnesses. Founded in Germany as the International Bible Students' Association, it early made its way to America. One of its first American leaders was Charles Taze Russell. He wrote a six-volume set known as *Studies in the Scriptures,* in which he carried the unorthodox ideas even further from the truth than the old International Bible Students' Association had done. In America the cult became known as Russellism. It was also sometimes called Millennial Dawnism.

Judge Rutherford (who never was really a true judge) arose within the ranks of this heresy and became its most brilliant and fluent interpreter. He and others renamed their movement Jehovah's Witnesses. As someone has remarked, "They are in reality Jehovah's *false* witnesses." The *Watchtower* publications have poured out millions of books and papers that have spread this false doctrine over the English-speaking world and into other lands.

About 1844, there arose the beginnings of the Seventh Day Adventist movement. This group is quite orthodox except in respect to the notion that the soul "sleeps" in the grave between death and the judgment. Following the judgment, they hold that the wicked will become extinct through annihilation. The Adventists have spread over much of the world as missionaries for their cause.

There are several central errors about the dead in these false theories.

1. *The soul and death.* Rutherford said, "No man has a soul. The preachers have made people believe that man carries a soul around with him and that when he dies the soul hikes off to some other place."

Russell's definition of death was "a period of absolute nonexistence." Rutherford said of sinners, "They are entirely unconscious in the grave. They are not suffering because they do not exist." Seventh Day Adventists teach that the state to which sinners are reduced is one of "silence, inactivity, and entire unconsciousness."

2. *Resurrection, second chance, and hell.* Jehovah's Witnesses maintain that all men will be resurrected and given a second chance at salvation during the millennium. The second trial will be more favorable than the first. If such characters as even Nero, who had Paul beheaded, repent and turn to God during this second chance, they may become shining models of righteousness. (See Russell's *Studies in the Scriptures,* 1:106-7, 111, 129, 143; 6:178.)

3. *Hell.* These teachings assert that God is too good to sustain an everlasting hell (Russell, 1:127). The penalty for refusing the second chance of eternal life, after death, will be the "second death," which is total annihilation (Russell, 1:151). Hellfire is merely symbolic of the destroying of error and the purifying of faith (Russell, 1:320).

Death, which is the extinction of being, is the punishment for all willful sinners (Russell, 3:117).

# Man's Spiritual and Physical Natures

Man is at least a duality, possessed of body and spirit. Christian psychologists often think of him thus, while the theologians generally think of him as possessing body, soul, and spirit. Soul and spirit for the psychologist are the same thing; for the theologian, they are separate entities of man's nature. The Greek words for body, soul, spirit, and mind are all separate terms with distinctive meanings.

By *soul* is generally meant those conscious qualities of sight, sound, touch, taste, and smell, plus the awareness of one's selfhood. By *spirit,* we are to understand the higher part of mankind, such as intellect, self-willing, self-awareness, self-directiveness, the ability to reason, and the moral qualities. These belong to man in a sense in which they do not belong to animals. The animals feel, see, and taste; but they cannot reason, and they have no moral qualities. It is doubtful, too, whether they have self-awareness, beyond the mere sense of being alive. Animals have no true sense of any selfhood, as does man.

The Bible abundantly proves that man has two natures, physical and spiritual. These two are clearly distinguished from each other all through the Scriptures. Jesus emphasized this truth when He pointed out to Nicodemus the need for the new birth (see John 3:1-12).

Note in the following passages that the Scriptures teach that man has a spiritual nature, as distinguished from the body.

Job 32:8, "There is a spirit in man: and the inspiration of the Almighty giveth them understanding."

Zech. 12:1, "The Lord . . . stretcheth forth the heavens, and layeth the foundation of the earth, and formeth the spirit of man within him." The spirit within man and the body are as distinct as a house and a tenant within the house.

Job 14:22, "His flesh upon him shall have pain, and his soul within him shall mourn." Here the "flesh" and "soul" are distinct. The flesh is "upon him," or envelopes the soul; while the soul is "within him" or in the body. And these two, the "flesh" without and the spiritual nature within, constitute the man.

1 Cor. 2:11, "What man knoweth the things of a man, save *the spirit of man which is in him?* even so the things of God knoweth no man, but the Spirit of God" (italics added).

The biblical distinction between the body and the spirit is obvious. The above passage proves that man has a spiritual nature distinct from the body in which it dwells.

In Matt. 10:28, the spiritual nature is further distinguished from the body. Our Saviour teaches that the soul cannot be killed: "Fear not them which kill the body, but are not able able to kill the soul." It is evident that the soul is not the body, nor the body the soul. If those who are able to kill the body are not able to kill the soul, how can some say that the body and soul are the same?

The history of the first man shows conclusively that he was created as a compound being, a body and a spiritual nature. "The Lord God formed man of the dust of the ground, and breathed into his nostrils the breath of life; and man became a living soul" (Gen. 2:7). Mark the order of events.

1. The Lord God "formed man of the dust of the ground." This was of course a material nature—his body. There it lay, perfect in all its parts. Why could not the brain have thought, the nerves felt, the eyes seen, and the ears heard? Because the conscious spirit was not yet there. The man formed of the dust was as yet a mere lifeless body.

2. In the second step of creation, God "breathed into his nostrils the breath of life." This act was plainly the infusion of spiritual nature into the material body. The author of Literal Translation of the Hebrew renders the passage, "And Jehovah Elohim formed a very man of the dust of the ground, and blew into his nostrils the living spirit, and man was for a living creature." He was but a "body" before, but now he has become a "living soul."

The two following references also clearly establish the fact that man is a triune being:

1 Thess. 5:23, "I pray God your whole spirit and soul and body be preserved blameless unto the coming of our Lord Jesus Christ."

Heb. 4:12, "The word of God is quick, and powerful, and sharper than any twoedged sword, piercing even to the dividing asunder of soul and spirit, and of the joints and marrow, and is a discerner of the thoughts and intents of the heart."

We shall not attempt further to define the difference between "soul" and "spirit." They are not the same, but they are so closely related that it is difficult to accurately distinguish them.

In the Scriptures the words for "spirit" and "soul" are not always translated the same. Sometimes in the original where the word "soul" appears, it is translated by the English word "spirit." Then again, where the word for "spirit" appears, frequently it is translated by the English word "soul."

Because the words are so closely related and because they are so seldom distinguished, either of them is descriptive of, and is understood to mean, the entire spiritual nature of man. The two terms in the vocabulary of religious writings are generally synonymous. Therefore, hereafter in this book when we use either of the two words, we are speaking of man's spiritual being.

Judge Rutherford and those who adhere to his theory are unscriptural when they say that no man has a soul. He tries to get around the biblical evidence by asserting that wherever the word "spirit" is used in expressions such as "spirit within man" or "spirit in man," the word merely means "breath." Of course, at death, the breath passes out into space, and man is completely dead. It is true that the same Hebrew word can be translated as "spirit" and as "breath." But Bible scholars agree that the correct translation must be determined by the context. To settle on the same translation, no matter what the context, throws one into absurdity.

Notice Job 34:14-15, "If he set his heart upon man, if he gather unto himself his spirit and his breath; all flesh shall perish together, and man shall turn again unto dust." Here observe that the "spirit" and "breath" of man are two distinct things.

If "spirit" meant the same as "breath," the following predicament would result: "If he gather unto himself his *spirit* and his *spirit*," or, "If he gather into himself his *breath* and his *breath*."

As more evidence of this, see into what dilemma this system of interpretation would divert the Scriptures. In the following passages "breath" is substituted for "spirit" and printed in italics.

Acts 23:8, "The Sadducees say there is no resurrection, neither angel, nor *breath:* but the Pharisees confess both." Also verse 9, "If a *breath* or an angel hath spoken to him."

Rom. 2:29, "Circumcision is that of the heart, in the *breath.*" 1 Cor. 5:5, "To deliver such an one unto Satan . . . that the *breath* may be saved in the day of the Lord Jesus."

2 Cor. 7:1, "Let us cleanse ourselves from all filthiness of the flesh and *breath.*" Gal. 6:18, "The grace of our Lord Jesus Christ be with your *breath.*"

In the following passage the word "breath" is substituted for "soul" and likewise italicized.

Ps. 19:7, "The law of the Lord is perfect, converting the *breath.*" Ps. 106:15, "He gave them their request; but sent leanness into their *breath.*"

Matt. 10:28, "Fear not them which kill the body, but are not able to kill the *breath:* but rather fear him which is able to destroy both *breath* and body in hell." Luke 12:19, "I will say to my *breath, Breath,* thou hast much goods laid up for many years."

1 Thess. 5:23, "I pray God your whole spirit and *breath* and body be preserved blameless." Jas. 5:20, "Let him know, that he which converteth the sinner from the error of his way shall save a *breath* from death." 2 Pet. 2:8, "[Lot] vexed his righteous *breath* from day to day."

The Scripture teaches that man has a soul distinct from the body in which it dwells, so Rutherford's theory fails on its first point when tested in the light of the Holy Bible.

In addition to the convincing statements of Scripture, the following notes are worthy of our consideration. They are not submitted as evidence to prove that man has a soul, because this is a doctrinal truth based on Scripture. They are, however, of interest because they are in harmony with this biblical teaching.

The matter in our body is gradually and constantly changing. We are not the identical physical persons we were a few years ago. New cells are continually being added while other cells are continually being removed as waste products. After this process has continued for a period of several years, all the cells have been replaced. None of the old cells remain. This means that we have a new brain—an entirely different brain every few years.

It is a remarkable fact that while we have a new brain, yet memories remain. We can remember clearly events that occurred many years back. The brain has been changed many times, yet with an entirely different brain one is able to remember the experiences of previous years. What is the explanation to this phenomenon? There is but one; there is an indestructible spirit or spiritual nature in man.

It is the spirit, the real individuality, distinct from the body that remembers and remains long after the body has been changed many times. The spirit carries the memories and survives all the bodily changes. It is not the body but the spirit that thinks, wills, plans, remembers, and holds communion with God.

When a person dies, the brain, eyes, ears, and nerves are still the same members; yet the brain cannot think, the eyes cannot see, the ears cannot hear, the nerves produce no feeling. Why? Because it was not the body but the real spiritual nature within the body that did the thinking, seeing, hearing, and feeling.

The Associated Press once released an article from Dr. William Mayo, world-famous surgeon, at the Mayo Clinic in Rochester, Minn. Dr. Mayo said: "The keen blade of my scalpel may never uncover the soul as a tangible part of the mystery called man, but I know it is there. I am as confident of its presence as I am of the most elemental truth to which my own medical science adheres."

So we have conclusive biblical proof of the distinct difference between the body and the spirit of man. It is upon the spiritual nature of man that we base the teachings of eternal life for the righteous, and everlasting punishment for the wicked. Because man has the qualities of eternal duration, he demands treatment as an eternally enduring being. His very nature cries out for everlasting existence; this existence becomes the basis of his morals and of his treatment as a moral being.

# CHAPTER 4

# What Is Death?

What is the scriptural meaning of death? Is it the total extinction of life, or is it merely the cessation of physical life? Nature itself cannot provide the answer, nor can speculation or philosophy. When animals die, it is apparently the total extinction of that animal's life, but is this so with man? Does not man have something higher about him, something which he received at the beginning of life that indicates survival after death?

From the creation of Adam it is seen that his life began with the union of physical and spiritual life (see Gen. 1:27; 2:7). Death, for man, therefore, must be a *separation* of these two vital factors—the spirit leaves the body, which returns to its clay. The Scriptures bear out this fact.

The original decree of death (Gen. 3:19) implies only the death of the body. "In the sweat of thy face shalt thou eat bread, till thou return unto the ground; for out of it wast thou taken: for dust thou art, and unto dust shalt thou return." Here it is plain that only so much of man as was "dust," and taken out of the ground, was destined to return to dust again. But the "breath of life" breathed into Adam by his Creator was not dust nor was it taken out of the ground. It, therefore, was not to return to dust with the body at death.

Wherever the fulfillment of this original decree is spoken of in the Scriptures, it is described as taking effect upon the body only. The spirit is released from the body and survives its dissolution. According to the Bible, death is a separation of the spirit from the body.

Eccles. 8:8 reads, "There is no man that hath power over the spirit to retain the spirit; neither hath he power in the day of death." This passage clearly refers to death; and the expression "to retain the spirit" clearly implies that in death the spirit *departs from the body*. It cannot be "retained" either by burial of the body or by any other means.

Eccles. 12:7 says, "Then shall the dust return to the earth as it was: and the spirit shall return to God who gave it." The allusion to Gen. 3:19 is unmistakable. The "dust" or body only is to "return to the earth as it was" while the spirit returns unto God who gave it.

That death is a separation of the soul from the body is clearly implied in 1 Kings 17:20-22, where Elijah prayed that the son of the widow of Zarephath might be restored to life. "He cried unto the Lord, and said, O Lord my God, hast thou also brought evil upon the widow with whom I sojourn, by slaying her son? And he stretched himself upon the child three times, and cried unto the Lord, and said, O Lord my God, I pray thee, let this child's soul come into him again. And the Lord heard the voice of Elijah; and the soul of the child came into him again, and he revived."

When the ruler's daughter was raised to life (Luke 8:49-55), it is said, "Her spirit came again, and she arose straightway," implying that in dying her spirit had left the body and must needs come again before she could be restored to life. No language could make it more clear that death is a separation of the spirit from the body.

When David learned that his beloved child was dead (2 Sam. 12:19-23), he ceased to weep and fast. When questioned concerning his unusual conduct, he said, "Now he is dead, wherefore should I fast? can I bring him back again? I shall go to him, but he shall not return to me." This plainly indicates that his child had gone hence, and that he could not return. The bereft father expected to depart also—to "go to him"—when mortal life should end.

The Apostle Paul sets forth this same truth: "We are always confident, knowing that, whilst we are at home in the body, we are absent from the Lord: (for we walk by faith, not by sight:) we are confident, I say, and willing rather to be absent from the body, and to be present with the Lord. Wherefore we labour, that, whether present or absent, we may be accepted of him" (2 Cor. 5:6-9).

Death, as a separation, is inferred also in the following figure. The inspired writers represent the human body as a "tabernacle" or frail dwelling place, and death as the putting off of this tabernacle. Paul says, "We know that if our earthly house of this tabernacle were dissolved, we have a building of God, an house not made with hands, eternal in the heavens" (2 Cor. 5:1).

The Apostle Peter adds, "I think it meet, as long as I am in this tabernacle, to stir you up by putting you in remembrance; knowing that shortly I must put off this my tabernacle, even as our Lord Jesus Christ hath shewed me. Moreover I will endeavour that ye may be able after my decease to have these things always in remembrance" (2 Pet. 1:13-15).

In these passages, then, the "tabernacle" to be dissolved, and the dwellers in the tabernacle are as distinct as the house and its occupant. We are in a tabernacle, and death is the putting off of our tabernacle. Death is the separation of soul and body.

Various references speak of death as a departure. This shows that death is a separation of the spiritual nature from the body. Paul described death as a *departure* to occur when he should cease to abide in the flesh (Phil. 1:21-24). "To me to live is Christ, and to die is gain. But if I live in the flesh, this is the fruit of my labour: yet what I shall choose I wot not. For I am in a strait betwixt two, having a desire to depart, and to be with Christ; which is far better: nevertheless to abide in the flesh is more needful for you" (Phil. 1:21-24). What does the apostle here mean by "abiding in the flesh" if it be not living in the body? And what by "departing" if it be not dying? It is scarcely possible for language to teach more clearly the doctrine that death is a separation of body and spirit, and a departure of the spirit from this world.

The same doctrine is taught in numerous other scriptures. The apostle says, "I am now ready to be offered, and the time of my departure is at hand" (2 Tim. 4:6). Also in Gen. 35:18 we read, "It came to pass, as her soul was in departing, (for she died)." It was revealed to Simeon that he should not see death till he had seen the Lord Christ. When he saw the infant Redeemer, he said, "Lord, now lettest thou thy servant depart in peace, according to thy word."

That death is a separation of the soul from the body is further evident from Jas. 2:26, "As the body without the spirit is dead, so faith without works is dead also."

In the foregoing paragraphs, according to the testimony of the infallible Word of God we learn that death is a separation of the spirit, or the departure of the real individual, from the body.

The original decree of death consigns only the body to return to the earth, while the "spirit returns to God who gave it." Death is "the giving up of the ghost," and the dead are not restored to life, unless their "souls come into them again." We are now dwelling in "earthly houses of this tabernacle" which we shall "put off" at death. We now "abide in the flesh," but at death we will "depart" and will be absent from the body; then "the body without the spirit will be dead."

These scriptures show conclusively that there is a distinct separation of the body and spirit of man at death. Nowhere does the Bible set forth the idea that in the death of animals there is any such experience. Animals have no spirit or spiritual nature, and they therefore perish totally in the hour of death. But since man is a higher being, his spirit survives the crisis of natural death to the body and he lives on somewhere.

# Where Do Departed Spirits Dwell?

Mankind has sought throughout the centuries to find out where the departed spirits of men have gone. There has been in all literature the feeling that their loved ones did not cease to exist when they died; but that they "went somewhere."

That there is a spiritual nature or a soul in all men, and that this soul departs from the body in death is a clear biblical teaching. This has also been believed even by the heathen from the most ancient times, as may be seen in their burial rites and in the inscriptions on ancient tomb walls.

But where does the released spirit of man go when it leaves the body? Does it roam about in space, endlessly seeking some form of habitation? Or, does it go to some settled place of abode? Here I have largely followed Karl Sabiers in his famous book, *Where Are the Dead?*

First, it can be emphatically stated that the spirits of the departed do not roam about in space. The Bible makes it clear that there is a definite abode for them.

In order to get a correct understanding of the subject, it will be necessary to distinguish between the *past, present,* and *future* abodes of the dead. We must also look at the words as they are used in the original Hebrew and Greek texts and not as the translators have rendered them in our English versions. It would be impossible to arrive at an accurate understanding of death, heaven, and hell, from the English translations alone. The following scriptures as rendered in the King James Version, illustrate the predicament:

Christ said, "The rich man also died, and was buried; and in hell he lift up his eyes" (Luke 16:22-23). The original word *(hades)* is here translated "hell." In Matt. 23:33 Christ said, "Ye serpents, ye generation of vipers, how can ye escape the damnation of hell?" Here the original word *(gehenna)* is also translated "hell." In 2 Peter 2:4 we read, "If God spared not the angels that sinned, but cast them down to hell." Here the original word *(tartarus)* is also rendered "hell." The terms *hades, gehenna,* and *tartarus* are three different Greek words; they are names of three different places, but are all translated by the English word "hell." One can readily see why it is necessary to go direct to the original text to arrive at a correct understanding of the subject.

Now let us turn our attention to a similar situation in the Old Testament. When Jacob thought his son Joseph was devoured by a wild beast, he said, "I will go down into the grave unto my son mourning" (Gen. 37:35). Here the original word is *sheol* and is rendered "grave" by the translators. In Ps. 16:10 we read, "Thou wilt not leave my soul in hell." Here again is the same original word *sheol,* but this time it is not translated "grave," but is rendered "hell." Again, concerning the wicked who die, it says, "They go down quick into the pit" (Num. 16:30). Here again, in the original, is the same word *sheol,* but this time it is translated neither "grave" nor "hell," but "pit."

The Bible makes it clear that the place of the departed

dead is called *sheol* in the Old Testament Hebrew, but not always with exactly the same meaning. The word is found 65 times in the Old Testament. Thirty-one times it is translated "hell," 31 times "grave," and is three times translated "the pit." We cannot fairly charge the translators with carelessness, because the original word was obviously used by the Hebrews in several senses. Wiley writes: "The word sometimes means indefinitely, the grave, or place or state of the dead; and at others, definitely, a place or state of the dead into which the element of misery and punishment enters: but never a place or state of happiness, or good after death" (*Christian Theology,* 3:225). Under these conditions the translators must decide from the context of the passage which meaning of *sheol* is intended.

The Old Testament Hebrew word *sheol* for the place of the departed dead was translated in the Septuagint (Greek translation of the Old Testament) as *hades.*

Perhaps some sincere seeker for the truth is saying, "How do you know that the word *sheol* in the Old Testament Hebrew means the same as *hades* in the New Testament Greek?"

It was prophesied of Jesus that His soul should not remain in *sheol* and that His body should not see corruption. "Thou wilt not leave my soul in hell *[sheol];* neither wilt thou suffer thine Holy One to see corruption" (Ps. 16:10). This same verse is quoted in the New Testament Greek. "Thou wilt not leave my soul in hell *[hades],* neither wilt thou suffer thine Holy One to see corruption" (Acts 2:27).

Here is strong evidence that the Hebrew word *sheol* has the same meaning as the Greek word *hades.* This same verse is written with *sheol* in the Hebrew and *hades* in Greek. Both mean the abode of the spirits of the departed dead.

Judge Rutherford, and those who adhere to his theory, would like us to believe, that *sheol* and *hades* is not the place of departed spirits, but always mean the grave where the bodies are laid. He declares that *sheol* means the grave —the condition of death, not the abode of spirits.

But this is not so. The abode of departed spirits is one place, and the grave is another. They are not the same. However, as we have seen, *sheol* sometimes refers to one and sometimes to the other; both uses are present in the Old Testament, therefore the context must always be studied to determine the exact meaning of the term.

The following considerations furnish further proof of the distinction between the abode of the departed spirits and the grave, the resting place of the body.

1. In both the Hebrew and Greek languages, there are other words than *sheol* and *hades* that refer to the places of the dead. The Hebrew word for the grave into which only the bodies of the dead go, is *queber.* The Greek parallel is *mnemeion.* These are used many times in the Scriptures.

2. The word *sheol* is never used in the plural, suggesting that it is one place; *queber,* on the other hand, is used many times in the plural; there are, of course, many graves.

3. We never read of a person having a *sheol,* but we often read of a person having a *queber.*

4. The body is never said to be in *sheol* and the spirit is never to be in the grave.

5. No *sheol* was ever dug by man or was ever located on the earth, but this can be said of graves. The Scriptures distinguish clearly enough between the abode of the spirits and the resting place for the body. Both are recognized by biblical writers.

6. In the final judgment, both the *grave* and *hades*

will deliver up the dead. "Death [the grave] and hell *[hades]* delivered up the dead which were in them" (Rev. 20:13).

7. Christ has the keys of both. "I am alive for evermore, Amen; and have the keys of hell *[hades]* and of death [the grave]" (Rev. 1:18).

8. Christ's soul was not left in *hades,* neither was His body left in the tomb (Acts 2:27). Here again the grave is clearly distinguished from *hades.*

9. When Jacob's sons sold Joseph into Egyptian slavery, they deceived their father by bringing to him Joseph's blood-stained coat, making him think that a wild beast had devoured Joseph. Jacob's sons and daughters tried to comfort him, but he would not be comforted. He said, "I will go down into the grave unto my son mourning" (Gen. 37:35).

The original word in the Hebrew is *sheol.* Judge Rutherford asserts that here *sheol* is the grave, the place where bodies are laid. He says, "It is easy to be seen that Jacob expected to go to the tomb." But from what Jacob thought and said, we can see that he did not intend to go into the tomb to meet his son Joseph, but into the abode of the departed spirits. We know that Jacob did not believe that Joseph was in the grave, for he believed that a "wild beast" had devoured him (verse 33). Therefore it would have been impossible for Jacob to go to the grave to meet Joseph; where he really intended to meet him was the abode of the spirits of the departed dead.

10. Jacob is said to have been gathered unto his people at the moment of death, though his body was not buried with the bodies of his ancestors till months afterward. "When Jacob had made an end of commanding his sons, he gathered up his feet into the bed, and yielded up the ghost, and was gathered unto his people" (Gen. 49:33).

Jacob died in Goshen in Egypt but was buried in the land of Canaan. They were 40 days embalming the body, and the mourning in Egypt continued 30 days longer. Joseph then obtained permission of Pharaoh to go and bury his father (50:3-6). How long they journeyed is not stated, but they mourned seven days more at the threshing floor of Atad (50:10), so that at least 80 days elapsed between the gathering unto his people and the burial of the body in the cave of Machpelah in Canaan.

Jacob was "gathered unto his people" at the time of his death, by the departure of his soul to the souls of Isaac, his father, and Abraham, his grandfather. Therefore his gathering to His people was not to their bodies in the graves but to the place where they were in their disembodied state.

These 10 considerations show that Judge Rutherford and those who believe in his theory are wrong when they say that *sheol* and *hades* always mean the grave. The terms are often used to describe the abode for departed spirits.

In studying its location, we find that in 20 of the 65 Old Testament passages that refer to *sheol*, it is located downward. Jacob said, "I will go down [into *sheol*]" (Gen. 37:35). In New Testament references to *hades*, we also find that it is located downward. "Thou . . . shalt be brought down to *[hades]*" (Matt. 11:23); "Thou . . . shalt be thrust down to *[hades]*" (Luke 10:15). Never do we find the Scriptures locating *sheol* or *hades* on earth or above the earth, but always downward.

### Sheol

Thus far nothing has been said relative to the righteous and the unrighteous in *sheol*. It has been merely stated that the spirits of all the dead, regardless of moral distinction, righteous or unrighteous, departed to *sheol*.

The Old Testament sheds very little light on the subject. It merely tells that all the dead go to *sheol*. It makes no distinction between abodes for the saved and the lost. In the Old Testament, the light on the state of the departed dead is in the twilight stage.

Why is it that the Old Testament is thus almost silent on the future state? Why does it leave us with so little information? The Bible clearly answers that question. The time for the revealing of the conditions beyond the grave had not yet come in Old Testament days. It was reserved for Christ to "bring life and immortality to light through the gospel" (2 Tim. 1:10).

And that is just what Christ did. The Old Testament teaching which is in the twilight stage on immortality and conditions in *sheol,* is now made manifest by Christ through the gospel. Scripture does not say that when Christ came, He brought life and immortality into existence, but that He brought it to light—He revealed it.

Since Christ has brought immortality to light, we must accept His statements. We should learn what His teaching was regarding the conditions in the abode of the departed dead.


### Hades

The account of the rich man and Lazarus (Luke 16:19-31) gives us a description of the abode of the departed dead as it was in the Old Testament days and in the days of Christ's earthly ministry.

Lazarus died and the rich man also died, and his body was buried, but in hell *(hades)* he was suffering "torment" (v. 23). The word is used five times in the account. Notice that the rich man was in a "place," not merely a "state"; verse 28 says "this place of torment." From there he saw in the distance Abraham, and also Lazarus who was being comforted (vv. 23, 25). Thus, in *hades,* according to Christ's teaching, there was a "place of torment" for the unrighteous, and a place of comfort for the righteous. These two places, the place of comfort and the place of torment, were separated by a great gulf fixed, so that no one could pass from one place to the other (v. 26).

Acts 2:27, which speaks of Christ, says, "Thou will not leave my soul in hell *[hades].*" Here it is clearly indicated that Christ's soul went to *hades* after His death on the Cross, but it does not say to which of the two compartments in *hades* His soul went. When we associate this statement with Christ's promise to the penitent thief on the Cross, the meaning is clear. Christ said, "Today thou shalt be with me in paradise" (Luke 23:42). When Christ and the penitent thief went to *hades,* they did not go to the "place of torment"; Christ said they both were to be in "paradise." This paradise must have been the place of comfort, called "Abraham's bosom."

This is what Christ revealed of *hades* as it was in the Old Testament times and in the days of His earthly ministry, but we find a great change took place when Christ ascended.

### *Hades as It Is Now*

The Scripture reveals that since Christ's resurrection and ascension the section in *hades* known as "Abraham's bosom" or "paradise" is no longer the abode for the spirits of the righteous dead.

As previously stated, before the Resurrection and Ascension, *hades* or *sheol,* the spirit-world, is represented as being below. Into it all the dead, both saved and lost, are said to have descended. Following Christ's resurrection and ascension, *hades* is never mentioned as the abode of redeemed spirits. Thereafter, the spirits of the righteous instead of descending are spoken of as going up.

1. In 2 Corinthians, Paul relates his experiences of being "caught up to the third heaven" and "caught up into paradise" (12:2, 4). According to this account, "paradise" and the "third heaven" have the same location. The abode of the righteous spirits is "up" and it is "in the third heaven." When did this change take place?

2. Paul tells us that before Christ ascended up into heaven, "He also descended first into the lower parts of the earth" (Eph. 4:9). When He ascended, did He go alone? No. He brought a multitude with Him. He took along the waiting spirits of the paradise section of *hades*. The Scripture says, "When he ascended up on high, he led captivity captive." The marginal reading is "He led a multitude of captives." Mark 16:19 and other scriptures tell us that Christ ascended into the heavens to the right hand of God, and this account in Ephesians tells us that He brought a multitude with Him.

3. There is still more evidence that paradise, the abode for the righteous spirits, has been changed, and is no longer below in *hades*. We are positive that the righteous dead are no longer in *hades*, because we know that they are with Christ where He is.

Paul declared that he desired to "depart to be with Christ" (Phil. 1:23). He was a righteous man, and he knew that to depart in death was "to be with Christ." And in 2 Cor. 5:6-8, Paul uses strong words expressing his confidence that to be "absent from the body" in death is to be "present with the Lord." The righteous dead are "with Christ"—they are "present with the Lord," therefore they must be where Christ is.

Now then where is Christ? Is He in *hades?* We know that the Scripture says of Christ (Acts 2:27) His soul was not left in *hades* (Acts 2:27). Dozens of other scriptures tell us that He has ascended into the heavens and is at the right hand of God. Inasmuch as the departed spirits of the righteous are present with the Lord, they must be where He is—*up in heaven,* not down in the section of *hades* known as "Abraham's bosom" or "paradise."

These evidences show that "paradise," the abode of the righteous, is no longer in *hades.* Since the ascension of Christ, the abode of the righteous is in "the third heaven," "with the Lord." *Sheol-hades* will never be the abiding place of any true saint of this age. The reason the Old Testament righteous went to *sheol-hades* was because their sins were not yet put away (Heb. 10:4). The Scripture says, "Now once in the end of the world [ages] he hath appeared to put away sin by the sacrifice of himself" (Heb. 9:26). When the sins of the Old Testament righteous were "put away" by Christ's sacrifice on Calvary, they could enter into the very presence of God as do the spirits of the righteous of this age.

Paradise, the present abode of the righteous, must not, however, be confused with the final heaven, the New Jerusalem, which is still future.

The spirits of the lost, the wicked dead, still go to *hades* into "the place of torment." No change in their abode has been revealed in the Scripture. They are still in *hades,* and all the spirits of the unrighteous who shall die in the future will also go there. We know that this is true because of the great white throne judgment at which the wicked are to appear. We read that "hell *[hades]* delivered up the dead" (Rev. 20:13). *Hades* is still the abode of the unrighteous, and it will continue to be until the time of the great white throne judgment. At that time the spirits of the wicked will be brought up out of *hades.*

### The Three Heavens

The word "heaven" is used in the Bible in three distinct, yet closely related, senses.

1. In Acts 14:17, we read of the heaven of the earth's atmosphere: "God gave us rain from heaven." This is the region of the clouds.

2. A second meaning is the "high places" of Satan's kingdom where the "principalities and powers" of evil dwell. "We wrestle not against flesh and blood, but against principalities, against powers, against the rulers of the darkness of this world, against spiritual wickedness in high places" (Eph. 6:12).

3. The "third heaven" or "heaven of heavens" is the place of God's throne and dwelling. We read, "Thou hast made heaven, the heaven of heavens, with all their host" (Neh. 9:6), and "the throne of the Majesty in the heavens" (Heb. 8:1). It was this third heaven to which Paul was caught up (2 Cor. 12:2-4). He calls it both the "third heaven" and "paradise," therefore the two must be the same, or paradise is a part of the third heaven. It is of this place that it is said, "There is joy in heaven over one sinner that repenteth" (Luke 15:7).

### Where Is the Throne of God?

Where is heaven? Spiritually speaking, it is just a little way. To be absent from the body is to be present with the Lord. As someone has expressed it, "It is near enough that God can hear us when we pray."

The location of the throne of God is significant. Jesus arose in a body of flesh and ascended to heaven; He is now living in heaven in that body. And the dead in Christ are now absent from the body and present with the Lord. This means that heaven is somewhere in particular—not just everywhere in general.

Many scriptures testify that Jesus is ascended up into heaven and is seated on the right hand of God. His ascension is told in Mark 16:19; Luke 24:51; and Acts

1:9-11. Christ is now seated "on the right hand of the throne of the Majesty in the heavens" (Heb. 8:1). He is there to appear in the presence of God for us (Heb. 9:24), and He is interceding for us (Heb. 7:25). Stephen, when dying, saw the heavens opened and saw Christ at the right hand of God (Acts 7:55-60).

Paradise and the throne of God are very closely associated. Paradise, the abode of the righteous, must have the same location as the throne of God. Is is plain that both are together, because Christ is said to be at the right hand of the throne of God; and the righteous dead are also said to be with Christ. This places the throne of God in the third heaven, because that is where the righteous are—in paradise, which is the third heaven.

Thus we know that paradise and the throne are in the third heaven—somewhere above the other two heavens. It must be a place, because Jesus is there in His bodily presence; it is at the right hand of the throne of God; and it is in the presence of the righteous in paradise.

The Scriptures always speak of heaven as "up." But which way is up? If we say it is in the direction at a right angle with the earth's surface wherever we may happen to be, it would be in a different direction from every point on the earth. From North America and from India it would be in virtually opposite directions.

The following scriptures may help us. We read of Lucifer (Satan): "Thou hast said in thine heart, I will ascend into heaven, I will exalt my throne above the stars of God: I will sit also upon the mount of the congregation, in the sides of the north: I will ascend above the heights of the clouds; I will be like the most High" (Isa. 14:13-14). Here we are told that heaven is above the clouds, above the stars, and "in the sides of the north" or "in the uttermost parts of the north" (ASV).

God says in Ps. 75:2, 6, "When I shall receive the congregation I will judge uprightly. . . . Promotion cometh neither from the east, nor from the west, nor from the south." Here it is implied that the throne of God, where He receives the congregation and judges uprightly, is in the north.

North is in the same direction from every point on our earth's surface; it is the same from China as from America, the same from the Antarctic as from the Artic. In our way of reckoning, north is "up" from everywhere on the earth.

When "the glory of Jehovah" visited the prophet Ezekiel, it came with a whirlwind "out of the north" (Ezek. 1:4-28).

In the northern heavens, the telescope reveals an apparently empty space where there are no stars, though the region all around is thickly dotted with them. Some astronomers say that this is a "rift in the sky." It may be wondered if the Holy Spirit had reference to this when He recorded, "He stretched out the north over the empty place, and hangeth the earth upon nothing" (Job 26:7). "Up" . . . "north" . . . "empty place" . . . we can only conjecture.

### In Summary

Let us again consider Judge Rutherford's theory which teaches that "no man has a soul"; that at death man becomes unconscious and passes entirely out of existence. We have shown that such a teaching is contrary to Scripture. The Bible teaches that man has a soul, and that at death the soul separates from the body. The spirits of the unrighteous depart to a place prepared for them in *hades,* and the spirits of the righteous, since the resurrection and ascension of Christ, depart to paradise, the third heaven.

The Jehovah's Witnesses use several scriptures trying to disprove that the spirits of the righteous are in the presence of Christ. They point out that the Bible says, "No man hath ascended up to heaven, but he that came down from heaven" (John 3:13). They also use Acts 2:34, "David is not ascended into the heavens."

Let us consider first John 3:13, "No man hath ascended up to heaven, but he that came down from heaven." Christ uttered this statement *before* His death, resurrection, and ascension. At that time, the spirits of the righteous were in *hades*. It was not until His ascension that the righteous were transferred to the third heaven. At the time Christ uttered His statement, no man had yet ascended to heaven. Therefore this statement is not contradictory to the fundamental teaching above.

Even if this statement had been uttered after the ascension and after the abodes had been changed, it would not contradict the orthodox teaching. The word "man," in the light of the context, refers to the body; and in this sense, no man has ascended to heaven, because the resurrection of the body has not yet taken place.

Further, let us consider Acts 2:34, "David is not ascended into the heavens." This passage, like the first, offers no opposition against the orthodox teaching that the righteous are in the third heaven. The whole drift of the context shows that Peter was speaking of David's body and not of his soul.

The subject under discussion here is the resurrection of Christ. God raised Jesus up bodily, and He is ascended and exalted by the right hand of God. But this is not true of David: "David is not ascended [bodily] into the heavens."

We have seen here that the righteous dead go immediately into paradise to be with Christ, but that the spirits of the wicked go into *hades,* or hell, there to remain until the resurrection of the unjust at the judgment day. These things the Scriptures clearly teach.

# CHAPTER 6

# The Annihilation Theory and Scripture

Man has always sought to delay or avoid just punishment for his sins. Even in Eden, Adam passed the buck when asked about his first sin. As if to blame God, he said, "The woman whom thou gavest to be with me, she gave me of the tree, and I did eat" (Gen. 3:12). Man has never gotten over the impulse to find someone else to blame for his sins and failures.

He has also conjured up the pleasant theory that after death man's spirit ceases to exist. Some claim that the spirit sleeps in the grave, but after the resurrection all the wicked dead will be burned up in a frightful holocaust in which this earth will also perish. So men who have not been redeemed and saved will become extinct. Such is the theory of Adventism and other cults.

To the question, Is the spirit conscious after death? the Bible answer is an absolute yes. But before we examine the scriptural evidence, let us look at the arguments of these false theorists.

The error that physical death is cessation of all consciousness until the resurrection of the body, is usually called the theory of soul sleep. The theory is based principally upon a few Old Testament passages. Judge Rutherford writes: "Now what do the Scriptures say about the dead? Are they conscious or unconscious?" Then he gives the following passages: "For the living know that they shall die: but the dead know not any thing . . . Whatsoever thy hand findeth to do, do it with thy might; for there is no work, nor device, nor knowledge, nor wisdom, in the grave, whither thou goest" (Eccles. 9:5, 10). "The dead praise not the Lord, neither any that go down into silence" (Ps. 115:17).

According to Rutherford's theory these scriptures are supposed to prove that when man dies, he knows not anything—he has no knowledge or wisdom or memory; he is in a condition of silence, unconsciousness, and non-existence.

In answering this so-called scriptural proof propounded by Rutherford, we should remember what has already been said about the Old Testament being almost silent as to the future life. Without the full revelation of this truth as we have it since Christ revealed it through the gospel, the grave is often the limit of the Old Testament vision. The writers speak within the limits of their knowledge; they speak of the grave as a place where activities of life cease.

Futhermore, in the New Testament, where we should expect to find every doctrine of the Old Testament completed, it is clear that the dead, whether saved or lost, are in full consciousness. Therefore, if the doctrine of soul sleep were true, it would be completed in the New Testament; but unfortunately for Rutherford, the New Testament teaches consciousness beyond the grave.

Now let us consider one of the main scriptures that is used to try to prove that the dead are unconscious and nonexistent: "The dead praise not the Lord, neither any that go down into silence" (Ps. 115:17).

This passage, as quoted, stands alone. It is separated from the verses that precede and follow it. For correct understanding, we cannot take a verse of the Bible away from the surrounding verses and interpret it by itself; we must consider context. When this verse is put back in its context, and the following verse is added, the meaning is changed. "The dead praise not the Lord, neither any that go down into silence. But we will bless the Lord from this time forth and for evermore" (Ps. 115:17-18).

If the first of these two verses teaches that the dead are unconscious and have no knowledge of God, the second verse certainly contradicts the first. If the inspired Psalmist were to praise the Lord for evermore, he certainly expected to be alive and conscious, not unconscious and out of existence.

Eccles. 9:5, 10 has also been taken apart from its context. When we supply the italicized words that Rutherford left out, we find an altogether different meaning. *To him that is joined to all the living there is hope: for a living dog is better than a dead lion.* For the living know that they shall die: but the dead know not any thing, *neither have they any more a reward; for the memory of them is forgotten. Also their love, and their hatred, and their envy, is now perished; neither have they any more a portion for ever in any thing that is done under the sun.* . . . Whatsoever thy hand findeth to do, do it with thy might; for there is no work, nor device, nor knowledge, nor wisdom, in the grave, whither thou goest" (Eccles. 9:4-6, 10).

When we consider the words in italics, it is clear that this text has reference solely to what the dead can know, or do, or receive "under the sun." It is talking about what the dead can know or receive in this world. When a person dies, he has no more part in anything that is done here on earth. The omitted verses make it clear that our hope and interest in all things earthly is limited to this short and transitory life.

Remember that the vision of Ecclesiastes is limited to those things that may be seen and known in this world. The phrase "under the sun" is the key to the book and is found 29 times. Solomon declared that "under the sun" all things were vanity. He was giving his estimate of life from a worldly viewpoint. But when he rises above the sun in the last chapter, he sees things from a heavenly viewpoint. He there declares, "Then shall the dust [the body] return to the earth as it was: and the spirit shall return unto God who gave it" (Eccles. 12:7). His final position is that only the body goes to the grave and that the spirit returns to God.

It has been clearly shown that Rutherford's soul-sleep theory has no Old Testament foundation to stand upon. Now let us see what his New Testament claims are, and how they are supposed to support his scheme.

It is claimed that the words *dead* and *death* always imply unconsciousness and nonexistence. Therefore when a man is spoken of as dead, the meaning is that he is out of existence. But such an interpretation is not according to the Bible.

Certainly when the words are used with a spiritual meaning, they do not imply unconsciousness. Paul writes: "And you hath he quickened, who were dead in trespasses and sins" (Eph. 2:1). It does not mean that they were unconscious or out of existence; the unregenerate as well as the regenerate have conscious existence.

Again in Luke 15:24 we read that when the prodigal son returned, the father said, "This my son was dead, and is alive again." In 1 Tim. 5:6 we read, "But she that liveth in pleasure is dead while she liveth." These people were said to be dead in one sense of the word, and yet they had conscious existence.

Those who adhere to the soul-sleep theory also claim that the words "sleep," and "fell asleep," when used in reference to death, mean unconsciousness and nonexistence. But again we shall find that this is not so. Let us examine four instances.

1. In John 11:11-14 we read the words of Jesus, "Our friend Lazarus sleepeth; but I go, that I may awake him out of sleep. Then said his disciples, Lord, if he sleep, he shall do well. Howbeit Jesus spake of his death: but they thought that he had spoken of taking of rest in sleep. Then said Jesus unto them plainly, Lazarus is dead."

Here Jesus speaks of death as a sleep, but it is very plain that He is referring not to Lazarus' soul but to his body. Jesus said, "I go, that I may awake him out of sleep"; this He did by raising his body from the grave. Additional proof is found in the words of Martha, "By this time he stinketh." It was the body and not the soul of Lazarus that the disciples were thinking of as that which was asleep.

2. In Matt. 27:52 we are told that at the time of the resurrection of Jesus "many bodies" of the saints which had fallen asleep arose. The word "bodies," as used in this sentence, shows that the term "fallen asleep" does not refer to the souls of the dead.

3. In Acts 7:59-60, in the account of the stoning of Stephen, we are told that he "fell asleep." When Stephen was dying, he said in verse 59, "Lord Jesus, receive my spirit." Why should he utter such a prayer if the soul at death entered into a state of unconsciousness?

4. In 1 Cor. 15:15-20, it is revealed that Christ was "the firstfruits of them that slept." Here again the word "slept" clearly refers to the body and not to the soul, because the subject of this chapter is the resurrection of the body.

The word "sleep" used in reference to the dead always applies to the body. Nowhere in the Bible do we find that the soul separated from the body is said to be sleeping.

These scriptures confirm that the spirit of man after death is fully conscious. It is neither asleep nor non-existent. It is present to itself, fully conscious of its existence and of where it exists.

"Shall we sleep between death and the judgment?" asks Tertullian. "Why, souls do not sleep even when men are alive. It is the province of bodies to sleep."

# CHAPTER 7

# Consciousness After Death

As we have seen, the souls of the dead are fully conscious after death. The righteous go to the third heaven to be with Christ in paradise; the wicked, into hell there to await the resurrection of their bodies. That this state of the soul is one of full consciousness, let the Scriptures further demonstrate.

1. The consciousness of souls after death is clearly taught in the story Jesus told of the rich man and Lazarus (Luke 16:19-31). The rich man "died, and was buried; and in hell *[hades]* he lift up his eyes, being in torments. . . ." And the beggar died, and was "carried by the angels into Abraham's bosom." The obvious teaching is that though both had died, in their disembodied condition their souls were conscious. They could see, recognize each other, hear, talk, feel, and remember, being comforted or tormented after death.

There are those who claim that this is more than a parable but an authentic account—that our Lord is relating the true history of what happened to two men who once lived and died. "There was a certain rich man" and "there was a certain beggar named Lazarus." The use of proper names, they say, is not typical of Jesus' parables, nor did he begin with the usual "And he spake unto them a parable."

But being a parable would not take away from the lesson being taught. We know that a parable is an illustration told to make clear an obscure truth. To be true to its purpose, a parable must distinctly and accurately portray an otherwise obscure truth. In this case, the souls of the dead are presented as living, talking, remembering, being comforted or tormented after death. Language could scarcely teach the doctrine more plainly.

The fact that the soul lives and is conscious after death is plain also from Matt. 10:28: "Fear not them which kill the body, but are not able to kill the soul." The body can be killed, but the soul cannot. Killing the body does not kill the soul. Certainly the soul is alive and conscious after the death of the body.

The same truth is taught in the account of Christ's transfiguration; we are told that "there appeared unto them Moses and Elias talking with him [Christ]" (Matt. 17:3). We know that Moses died on Mount Nebo 1,400 years earlier: "Moses the servant of the Lord died there in the land of Moab, . . . and he [Jehovah] buried him in a valley in the land of Moab, over against Beth-peor: but no man knoweth of his sepulchre unto this day" (Deut. 34:5-6). Moses' body was dead and buried. Here then we have the spirit of Moses, with Christ and Elias on the summit of Mount Tabor, 1,400 years after his body had died.

One of the strongest passages in the Bible which shows that the souls of the dead are alive and conscious is Heb. 12:1. Hebrews 11 lists many of God's heroes from Abel to David and the prophets, who died in the faith. Referring to these faithful ones, Heb. 12:1 says, "Wherefore seeing we also are compassed about with so great a cloud of witnesses, let us lay aside every weight, and the sin which doth so easily beset us." The souls of the faithful dead are not unconscious and out of existence, but are living witnesses. The word used for "witnesses" *(marturon)* is from the same word that we find in Acts 1:8, "Ye shall be witnesses unto me." The word is used only of those who have life and conscious intelligence. The faithful dead are not out of existence; they are living, conscious witnesses.

The words "eternal life" are full of significance and are worthy of our consideration in this discourse on consciousness of souls after the death of the physical body. If a dying person has accepted Christ as his personal Saviour, he has eternal life. He is in present possession of that life. Jesus said: "He that believeth on the Son hath everlasting life" (John 3:36), and again, "He that heareth my word, and believeth on him that sent me, hath everlasting life" (John 5:24; see also 10:27-30).

Such eternal life cannot be destroyed by death; it cannot be broken by a period of nonexistence from death until resurrection.

Jesus said to Martha, "I am the resurrection, and the life: he that believeth in me . . . shall never die" (John 11:25-26).

Here is the assurance given by the Son of God for the dying believer, that he shall live forever because he is in possession of the eternal life that never comes to an end. That life flows on forever.

The fact that souls are alive and conscious after bodily death is plainly taught in Luke 20:27, 37-38. The Sadducees, a sect of the Jews, did not believe in life after death. They denied all future existence. Josephus, a Jewish historian who lived about that time, wrote, "The doctrine of the Sadducees is this, that souls die with the bodies" (Antiquities b. 28:4). Another secular source says of the Sadducees, "They take away the belief of the immortal existence of the soul, and the punishment and rewards of Hades" (War b. 8:14). In Acts 23:8 Luke tells us that "the Sadducees say that there is no resurrection, neither angel, nor spirit"; and in Luke 20:27, we read that the Sadducees "deny that there is any resurrection."

These Sadducees who denied that souls live after death, and who said that there will be no resurrection, came to Jesus intending to ridicule and make fun of the doctrine of the resurrection. Christ told them, "Now that the dead are raised, even Moses shewed at the bush" (Luke 20:37). God spoke to Moses out of the midst of the bush, and said, "I am . . . the God of Abraham, the God of Isaac, and the God of Jacob" (Exod. 3:6). Jehovah spoke to Moses from the bush 15 centuries before Christ was born in Bethlehem. Abraham had been dead 330 years, Isaac 225 years, and Jacob 198 years. Yet God declared himself to be the God of these three persons who had long been dead. He said, "I am the God of Abraham"—present tense. God was at that time the God of Abraham, Isaac, and Jacob; therefore these patriarchs must have still been alive.

Remember Christ was addressing the Sadducees who denied that the soul existed after death, and who said that there will be no resurrection. His purpose is clearly seen, in that the Sadducees accepted only the Pentateuch as the divinely inspired Word of God. Therefore if any life beyond the grave could be proved from the Pentateuch, their theory would be in ruins. Christ settled beyond a shadow of a doubt the question of consciousness and existence after death. He affirmed that God was still the God of those patriarchs and that they were not dead but still alive. He could not be the God of those who had no existence. The Scripture says, "After that they [the Sadducees] durst not ask him any question at all" (Luke 20:40).

Consciousness after death is also implied in 2

Corinthians. Paul uses strong words to express his confidence that to be absent from the body (in death) is to be present with the Lord. "We are always confident, knowing that, whilst we are at home in the body, we are absent from the Lord" (2 Cor. 5:6). In verse 8 he says, "We are confident, I say, and willing rather to be absent from the body, and to be present with the Lord. Wherefore we labour, that, whether present or absent, we may be accepted of him."

Paul was willing to be "absent from the body" to be "present with the Lord." Certainly he believed that in the presence of the Lord he would be conscious, for there could be no possible satisfaction in being unconsciously present with the Lord.

The same truth is taught in Phil. 1:21-24 where Paul says, "For me to live is Christ, and to die is gain. . . . For I am in a strait betwixt two, having a desire to depart, and to be with Christ; which is far better: nevertheless to abide in the flesh is more needful for you." How could Paul "be with Christ" after death, if he became unconscious and nonexistent? Would it be "gain" and "far better" to be cut off from conscious fellowship with God for perhaps centuries awaiting the resurrection? Paul desired to "depart, and to be with Christ," because he knew he could be conscious.

Luke 23:42-43 tells us that the dying thief upon the cross said to Jesus, "Lord, remember me when thou comest into thy kingdom. And Jesus said unto him, Verily I say unto thee, To day shalt thou be with me in paradise." The promise of the Saviour was that the thief should be with Him in paradise *that day*.

Those who do not believe in conscious existence after death try to do away with this clear evidence. They tell us that the sentence "Verily I say unto thee, To day shalt thou be with me in paradise" is not correctly punctuated.

They claim that the comma before the word "To day" should be placed behind it, to make the sentence read, "Verily I say unto thee to day, Shalt thou be with me in paradise." This completely changes the meaning, and makes the verse read as if Jesus had said, "I make it known to you today, that sometime in the future you shall be with Me in paradise." But this means an obvious distortion of our Lord's meaning.

Some say that paradise means the grave and that they met in the grave that day. If the Saviour simply meant to say that they would both soon be in the grave, it was no news to the thief. He already knew that he was going to die on the cross and that there was no escape from the grave. What better off was he who repented and prayed than he who railed and was forgotten? The passage cannot be successfully twisted to mean unconsciousness or nonexistence in the grave. It can have but one meaning. Christ and the thief met in the paradise section of *hades* and were conscious. Paradise signifies "pleasure" or "delight." These are emotions that demand consciousness. If the thief were not conscious of the presence of Christ in paradise, there could not possibly have been any comfort in the promise.

It is clear from the study of church history that the early Christians and martyrs understood the Scripture to teach the consciousness of the soul after death. It is certain that they looked for conscious joy in paradise immediately after death.

Of the thousands of Christian martyrs who sealed the truth with their blood during the first centuries of the Christian era, not one expressed in his last moments, so far as can be determined, the idea that his soul would die when the body was dissolved. On the contrary, all expressed the hope of immediate and conscious happiness after death. Such was the testimony of the first martyrs— it was the doctrine they learned from the apostles and from the Holy Scriptures. Research shows that during the first three centuries not one instance can be cited in which a Christian ever expressed any hope in his last hours other than that of entering at once upon the joys of conscious and endless life.

In the catacombs of Rome in which the bodies of the martyrs were buried during the first three centuries of the Christian era, the inscriptions on the tombs throw great light upon the faith of the Early Church. The following are samples of those inscriptions:

"In Christ, Alexander is not dead, but lives—his body rests in the tomb." "One who lives with God." "Gone to dwell with Christ." "Snatched home eternally."

It is worthy of note that the word *death* is never used in reference to even one of all this vast company of the departed.

To the martyrs who died it was death and immediate glory. And so it is with other believers. Among the millions of Protestant Christians who for hundreds of years have had the privilege to make the Bible their study, how very few have understood it to teach any other doctrine. They read the blessed Bible to learn the way to heaven, and they understood it to teach that death is merely the separation of the soul from the body, and that the souls of the righteous enter immediately into the conscious joys of paradise. In this faith they have lived, and in this hope they have died.

Were all the early saints and martyrs in error? Who can believe it? This glorious doctrine of the consciousness of souls after death has been the teaching of the Church throughout all its ages. Latter-day cults have tried to twist these passages and beliefs out of their settings for their own purposes, but they have failed. The true historic position of Christianity remains unchanged as it will until the end of time: "I believe in the life everlasting."

# CHAPTER 8

# The Righteous and Paradise

As we have seen from the Scriptures, the dead have a conscious existence. In their present spiritual state, both the righteous and the wicked are conscious.

Let us here look at the "spirits of just men made perfect," in their spiritual abode. Our English word *paradise* comes from the Persians through the Greek language. When Alexander the Great and his soldiers conquered ancient Persia, they found these people were great lovers of the outdoors. They had many areas laid out in special arrangements where there were trees, streams, and beautiful scenery similar to our large parks. The word that they used for these areas was *paradise*. The Greeks borrowed the term and embedded it in their language. We understand the word to mean a place of pleasure, delight, rest, and peace; it is the name that we use for the abode of the righteous after death.

Paul was positive that for a Christian to depart in death was to enter a condition "far better" than what we have known in this world (Phil. 1:21-24). The most outstanding fact revealed concerning the righteous in paradise is that they are "present with the Lord." What could be more wonderful than the blessedness of this experience?

The Scriptures shed some light on what it really means. In Christ's prayer for the Church, He says, "Father, I will that they also, whom thou hast given me, be with me where I am; that they may behold my glory" (John 17:24). At death, Christians go to be with Christ where He is, there to behold His glory. Could any experience be more blessed? Yet at times, we desire to have our loved ones back with us again. But if we truly understood what it means to be "present with the Lord" and to behold his glory, we would never seriously desire our loved ones to return from paradise to this earth.

In addition to what has already been noted, David writes, "In thy presence is fulness of joy; at thy right hand there are pleasures for evermore" (Ps. 16:11).

Truly it is a wonderful place to which the righteous have gone. This reference also adds proof that the departed dead are aware of their condition. They are consciously enjoying "fullness of joy" and "pleasures for evermore." Further evidence comes from Jesus himself who tells us, "I say unto you, that likewise joy shall be in heaven over one sinner that repenteth, more than over ninety and nine just persons, which need no repentance" (Luke 15:7).

When Paul was caught up into paradise, he heard such unspeakable and glorious things that he could not explain them. He saw such wonders that it was impossible for him to describe his experience (2 Cor. 12:1-4). It is certain that the souls of the righteous in paradise are in a wonderful place.

To the Apostle John, God revealed that those who die in the Lord, are blessed and resting: "Blessed are the dead which die in the Lord from henceforth: Yea, saith the Spirit, that they may rest from their labours; and their works do follow them" (Rev. 14:13).

The Greek word for "henceforth" is *aparti;* it means from this time on, immediately, now. Those who die in the Lord do not need to sleep in the grave or to be out of existence for perhaps thousands of years before their heavenly joys begin; they enter at once into blessedness.

Another verse that adds to the evidence of what we have already learned concerning the righteous in paradise is Ps. 116:15, "Precious in the sight of the Lord is the death of his saints." Certainly it would not be pleasing in the sight of the Lord to send His saints into oblivion or to put them out of existence until the resurrection. The death of the believer is precious to Him because it brings the spirit into a perfect and permanent communion with himself; because it is the beginning of a joyful and never-ending reunion; because for us it is freedom from mortal limitations; and because for us it is deliverance from the realm of Satan and sin.

We may briefly summarize what is revealed concerning the righteous in paradise. For the Christian to depart in death is to enter a place that is "far better" than we have known in this world. It is a place in which the righteous are "present with the Lord," a place where there is "fulness of joy," and "pleasures for evermore." Paradise is so wonderful and glorious that man cannot find words to explain it. It is "unspeakable," a place in which the righteous dead are blessed and at rest. The death of the Lord's saints is precious in His sight because it brings them to this place and is the beginning of a joyful and never-ending reunion with Him.

Often writers try to give details about paradise and heaven; they attempt to answer the myriad questions that the human spirit asks. The Bible, however, reveals few details; it carries the subject only to a certain point and no further. To go beyond what the Bible reveals is only to indulge in speculation and guesswork. It is probably better that the Bible reveals only limited information about paradise and heaven. Perhaps if we knew all about it we would not be content to remain here a single hour. It will be wonderful enough when we get there. Let us thank God for the foregleams He has given us.

Will we recognize loved ones in paradise? This has been a question of great concern to many people. The following considerations are worthy of our attention.

1. David, the inspired Psalmist, said regarding his son who had died, "I shall go to him, but he shall not return to me" (2 Sam. 12:23). Surely David knew he would recognize his son when he would go to him at death; if not, there would be no purpose in making the statement.

2. Christ said to the dying thief, "To day shalt thou be with me in paradise" (Luke 23:43). Certainly they expected to recognize each other, or the thief would have no consolation or comfort in the promise.

3. When Moses and Elijah appeared with Christ on the Mount of Transfiguration, they were recognized by the disciples without a formal introduction (Matt. 17:1-4). These men had departed from the earth centuries before; yet when they returned, they had sufficient of the earthly personality to be recognized by men who knew them only by their descriptions. If the disciples recognized Moses and Elijah when they appeared on this earth, certainly they would be able to recognize them in paradise.

4. In the account of the rich man and Lazarus, the rich man recognized both Abraham and Lazarus who were in paradise (Luke 16:22-23).

5. Since to be in paradise is "far better" than to be here, we may be sure that we shall not know less there than we know here. If we know loved ones here, surely we will know them there. Paul declares that there we shall not see "darkly" but "face to face." Now we "know in part," but there we shall know even as we are known (1 Cor. 13:12).

No doubt many wonder whether the righteous are able to speak with the Lord. That the redeemed are able to speak with Him with whom they are thus "at home" seems beyond doubt. We are able to speak to Him even here; surely those who are in His bodily presence will not be less privileged than we are.

Paul writes of his desire "to depart, and to be with Christ" (Phil. 1:23). He would not have desired to be with Christ if he did not expect to recognize and commune with Him.

As further evidence see Rev. 6:10 in which the tribulation saints who have died address the Lord: "They cried with a loud voice, saying, How long, O Lord, holy and true, dost thou not judge and avenge our blood on them that dwell on the earth?" This verse applies to the tribulation which is still future. However, if these saints will be able to address the Lord, why wouldn't those who are now in paradise be able to do the same?

*　　*　　*

It has been shown from the Scriptures that the righteous dead are conscious, and that they are in the presence of Christ in a condition "far better" than here. They are "blessed," having "fulness of joy" in this "unspeakable" place.

While all of this is true, still it can be said of them that they are in a condition of incompleteness. In paradise, man is said to be incomplete because at death the spiritual nature separates and leaves the physical body on earth. Before man can be complete again, he must get his physical body which will be resurrected. All the righteous are in paradise awaiting their resurrection bodies.

It should be carefully noted that no saint has yet entered the final heaven, nor is any sinner yet in the final hell. Paradise is not the final heaven for eternity. At death

60

the souls of the righteous go to this paradise in the presence of Christ, but not to the final heaven. This eternal heaven, which the saints will occupy after they receive their resurrection bodies, is described in the last chapters of Revelation and should not be confused with the present paradise, which the righteous occupy until the resurrection.

Paradise, then, is a temporary abode of the saints, pending the judgment of the righteous at the judgment seat of Christ (Rom. 14:10). The conclusion of all earthly affairs will take place at the great white throne judgment (Rev. 20:11-15). This will be the final judgment for the wicked and the settling of all the affairs of mankind's probation.

# CHAPTER 9

# The Two Resurrections

In order to understand the further studies of the judgment and eternal rewards, we need to have a clear concept of the two resurrections as taught in the New Testament.

The righteous in paradise are incomplete, just as the wicked in *hades* are also. In each case only the disembodied spirits are there, though fully conscious. The bodies which have moldered away in the dust must be brought back and reunited with the spirits to form the complete person as they were in life.

There are those who think of the resurrection of the dead as foolishness. They make all kinds of excuses for not believing in the literal resurrection of the body. Some say that it is unnecessary. Others assert that if all the dead that have ever lived were to be raised at one time, there would not be standing room. This is a silly argument, because it has been figured out that if every person since Adam were raised all at the same time, and if each were given a square yard to stand on, the throng would fill less than half the state of Texas.

Still others argue that bodies which have been cremated, or torn to pieces by explosives, or those decomposed in the grave, cannot possibly be restored. But the Bible says that nothing is impossible with God (Luke 1:37). Surely the Creator who formed these bodies in the first place can reassemble the components or recreate appropriate resurrection bodies. The Word of God declares that the dead will be resurrected. He who reveals the truth has power to perform the act.

The resurrection of the body is taught in the Old Testament. Job declares, "Though after my skin worms destroy this body, yet in my flesh shall I see God" (Job 19:26). Daniel prophesies, "And many of them that sleep in the dust of the earth shall awake, some to everlasting life, and some to shame and everlasting contempt" (Dan. 12:2).

The resurrection of the body was also taught by Christ himself: "Marvel not at this: for the hour is coming, in which all that are in the graves shall hear his voice, and shall come forth; they that have done good, unto the resurrection of life; and they that have done evil, unto the resurrection of damnation" (John 5:28-29).

Here our Lord taught the resurrection of both the righteous and the unrighteous. This teaching was echoed by the Apostle Paul: "And have hope toward God, which they themselves also allow, that there shall be a resurrection of the dead, both of the just and the unjust" (Acts 24:15).

At first glance it might appear that there will be only one resurrection in which the bodies both of the righteous and the unrighteous will be raised. However, this view is not supported by the Scripture. When the above passages are considered in the light of other references, it is clear that there will be two distinct resurrections, one for the righteous and one for the unrighteous, separated by a period of time.

An eminent Hebrew scholar interprets Dan. 12:2 as follows: "At that time many of the people shall awake (or be separated) out from among the sleepers in the earth dust. These who awake shall be unto life eternal, but those who do not awake at that time shall be unto contempt and shame everlasting." Those who will be resurrected out from among the rest of the dead will be those who "shall be found written in the book" (Dan. 12:1).

Phil. 3:11 also brings out the truth that not all the dead are resurrected at one time. Paul writes: "If by any means I might attain unto the resurrection of the dead." The literal translation is the resurrection "out of" the dead. He was speaking of the resurrection of the righteous who are to be raised out from among the rest of the dead, that is the wicked. The inference is that there will be an interval of time before the wicked are resurrected.

In 1 Cor. 15:22-24, Paul plainly shows that all the dead will not be resurrected at the same time. Speaking of how all shall "be made alive," he says, "But every man in his own order." Here the word that is translated "order" is a military word which means "band, rank, group." The meaning is, "But every man shall be raised in his own group or rank." The order is then given:

1. "Christ the firstfruits" (resurrection of Christ).

2. "Afterward they that are Christ's at his coming" (resurrection of the righteous—still in the future).

3. "Then cometh the end" (resurrection of the wicked).

They that are Christ's are to be raised; then sometime later come the others. The Greek word for "then" means next in order or sequence. Thus there will be an interval of time between the resurrection of them that are Christ's and the end. There has already been a period of 1,900 years since "Christ the firstfruits." The next event will be the resurrection of "they that are Christ's at his coming."

In Luke 14:14 Jesus also makes it clear that not all the dead will be raised in one general resurrection, but that there will be two. He said, "Thou shalt be recompensed at the resurrection of the just." This implies that there will be another resurrection for the rest of the dead— the wicked.

In Rev. 20:6, there is more evidence of two distinct resurrections: "Blessed and holy is he that hath part in the first resurrection: on such the second death [the fate of the wicked] hath no power, but they shall be priests of God and of Christ, and shall reign with him a thousand years." Verse 5 tells us, "The rest of the dead lived not again until the thousand years were finished."

Here we read of the first resurrection and of those in it who will be blessed and holy. The use of the word "first" implies that there is a second resurrection— namely, for the unrighteous. We also see that there is a period of 1,000 years between the two resurrections.

The Scripture seems clearly to teach that there will be two resurrections, one for the righteous and one for the wicked—and that there will be a period of 1,000 years between them.

The Bible testimony is that the righteous will be raised at the second coming of Christ. "I would not have you to be ignorant, brethren, concerning them which are asleep, that ye sorrow not, even as others which have no hope. For if we believe that Jesus died and rose again, even so them also which sleep in Jesus will God bring with him. For this we say unto you by the word of the Lord, that we which are alive and remain unto the coming of the Lord shall not prevent [precede] them which are asleep. For the Lord himself shall descend from heaven with a shout, with the voice of the archangel, and with the trump of God: and the dead in Christ shall rise first: then we which are alive and remain shall be caught up together with them in the clouds, to meet the Lord in the air; and so shall we ever be with the Lord" (1 Thess. 4:13-17).

From this passage we learn that when Christ descends from heaven from the throne of God and paradise, he will bring the righteous dead with Him. The righteous will come to earth to get their resurrection bodies because "the dead in Christ shall rise first." After the spirits of the righteous have been reunited with their bodies, that is, after the righteous dead are resurrected, "Then we which are alive and remain [meaning the living saints] shall be caught up together with them [the resurrected dead] in the clouds, to meet the Lord in the air, and so shall we ever be with the Lord."

Speaking of the same event, the raising of the righteous dead, and the changing of the living believers, Paul writes: "Behold, I shew you a mystery; We shall not all sleep, but we shall all be changed, in a moment, in the twinkling of an eye, at the last trump: for the trumpet shall sound, and the dead [in Christ] shall be raised incorruptible, and we [living saints] shall be changed" (1 Cor. 15:51). This refers only to those in Christ, and not to the ungodly.

The apostle goes on to say, "So when this corruptible shall have put on incorruption, and this mortal shall have put on immortality, then shall be brought to pass the saying that is written, Death is swallowed up in victory. O death, where is thy sting? O grave, where is thy victory?" (1 Cor. 15:54-55).

These statements can apply only to those who belong to Christ. Yes, "we shall all be changed," the "dead in Christ" as well as the righteous who are "alive and remain." Both the resurrected saints and those who are changed without dying shall be caught up "together . . . to meet the Lord in the air; and so shall we ever be with the Lord."

There are varying ideas about the judgment of believers. Some think of this judgment as being administered immediately at death. There are others (among them the postmillennialists) who believe that there is to be one great judgment that will take place at the end of the world when all mankind shall be judged as to destiny and rewards. But there are those who say that this latter view is incorrect. They hold that there is the prior judgment seat of Christ for the meting out of rewards to the saved.

The Christian's judgment as to destiny is past. Paul writes, "There is therefore now no condemnation to them which are in Christ Jesus" (Rom. 8:1). Jesus declared, "He that heareth my word, and believeth on him that sent me, hath everlasting life, and shall not come into condemnation; but is passed from death unto life" (John 5:24). The word translated "condemnation" means judgment. The believer's judgment as to *sin* is thus in the past. This judgment took place at Calvary's cross on the basis of Christ's finished work.

Paul writes of God's action, "He hath made him [Christ] to be sin for us, who knew no sin; that we might be made the righteousness of God" (2 Cor. 5:21; cf. Gal. 3:13; 1 Pet. 2:24). The sins of the believer have already been judged and put away. Thus Paul rightly says in 1 Tim. 5:24 that some men's sins are open beforehand and go before into judgment, and some men's sins follow after.

Though the believer's judgment as to sin is already past, the judgment of his works is still future. It will occur at the "judgment seat of Christ," which would appear to be something different from the "great white throne" judgment. The judgment of the believer is not to decide destiny but is for adjustment, reward, and perhaps position in the Kingdom. Every man shall be judged according to his works. It is the opinion of many that this judgment will take place after the "dead in Christ" are raised and the living believers are changed. This could be what Paul refers to when he writes, "We must all [those 'accepted of him'] appear before the judgment seat of Christ; that every one may receive the things done in his body, according to that he hath done, whether it be good or bad" (2 Cor. 5:10; cf. 1 Cor. 3:11-15).

In this connection, various crowns are referred to in Scripture as rewards: the crown of life (Jas. 1:12; Rev. 2:10); the crown of glory (1 Pet. 5:4); the crown of rejoicing (1 Thess. 2:19); the crown of righteousness (2 Tim. 4:8); the crown incorruptible (1 Cor. 9:25).

There are also still other events that will transpire before the righteous enter the final heaven to spend eternity. The great event will be "the marriage supper of the Lamb" (Rev. 19:7-9). The bride of Christ will be the true Church—those of the first resurrection, and the living believers who have been caught up and changed without dying.

It is believed that the great tribulation will take place on earth during the judgment of believers and the marriage of the Lamb. The climax of the terrible tribulation period will be the revelation of Christ, the *apokalupsis;* this is the other phase of Christ's second coming. These two phases are clearly distinguished in the Greek. The *parousia,* or corporeal appearing, is His coming for His saints. This will be the raising of the dead in Christ and the changing of the living believers. The *apokalupsis* (revealing, unveiling) is His coming with His saints following the believers' judgment and the marriage of the Lamb.

Following are some of the references in which the word *parousia* is found and translated "coming": Matt. 24:3, 27, 37, 39; 1 Cor. 15:23; 1 Thess. 2:19; 4:15; 5:23; 2 Thess. 2:1. Luke 17:34-36 and John 14:3 also refer to Christ's *parousia.*

Some verses that refer to the *apokalupsis* are Zech. 14:5; Col. 3:4; 2 Thess. 1:7-8; Jude 14; Rev. 1:7.

This revelation of Christ, His coming with His saints, will climax the tribulation period and usher in the millennial reign of Christ with His saints (Rev. 20:6). After this the earth will be renovated by fire (2 Pet. 3:10-13), and the New Jerusalem, the eternal abode for the righteous, will descend from heaven (Rev. 21:1-2).

# CHAPTER 10

# Resurrection Bodies

We have seen that the resurrection of the righteous will occur at Christ's return, and that the living believers will also be transformed and caught up with Him in the air. This tells us when the resurrection will occur.

Our next query would naturally be: What will the resurrection bodies of the saints be like? We are so deeply involved with our bodies in this life that it is only natural to be concerned about the bodies that we shall have for eternity. The Lord does not condemn us for this interest; rather He has responded to our concern by giving us some understanding.

The resurrection body will not be exactly like the physical body that goes into the grave. Paul said, "Thou sowest not that body that shall be" (1 Cor. 15:37). The resurrection body will far excel this earthly frame, but there must be an identity, or there could not be a true resurrection of that which went into the ground. This identity is not necessarily absolute sameness of substance. As noted in Chapter 2, we are not even the same physical persons we were several years ago. New cells are continually being added to our bodies, while others are being

70

removed as waste products. After this process has continued for a period of years, all the cells have been replaced. The body has been changed. It is an entirely new physical entity, yet memory and identity remain. So there will be great changes in the resurrection body, yet identity will remain.

In 1 Cor. 15:35 Paul asks, "How are the dead raised up? and with what body do they come?" He then answers the question by telling us what the resurrection body will be like. "It is sown in corruption; it is raised in incorruption" (v. 42). In verse 53 Paul adds, "For this corruptible must put on incorruption, and this mortal must put on immortality." The true word for "immortality" occurs in only three places in the New Testament; here in 1 Cor. 15:53-54, and in 1 Tim. 6:16.

At the resurrection of the righteous these corruptible bodies will be gloriously changed; the resurrected body will be incorruptible and immortal.

"Mortal" means perishable or subject to death; this is the nature of the physical body. "Immortal" means imperishable, not subject to death; such is the glorified body. Adam's body became mortal when he sinned, and this mortality passed upon all men.

At this place in our study it is important to clearly distinguish between "eternal existence," "eternal life," and "immortality." *All* persons have eternal existence, both saved and unsaved, whether in heaven or in hell. In contrast, eternal life is possessed only by those who have received Christ as their personal Saviour and have been born again. This term refers to receiving the spiritual nature of Christ in regeneration; and it carries with it the promise of continuing forever in heaven. Only those who accept Christ have the gift of eternal life.

The gift of immortality is closely related to eternal life, but it is not the same. Only those who have eternal life are eligible for immortality. They do not "put on" this immortality immediately at death, but the gift of eternal life entitles them to it. Immortality will be "put on" at the same time by all of the redeemed—at the resurrection of the righteous when Christ returns.

The following scriptures show that man is now mortal, and that Christ is the only One who has immortality. "This mortal must put on immortality" (1 Cor. 15:53). "When . . . this mortal shall have put on immortality" (1 Cor. 15:54). "Shall mortal man be more just than God?" (Job 4:17). "Let not sin therefore reign in your mortal body" (Rom. 6:12). "He that raised up Christ from the dead shall also quicken your mortal bodies" (Rom. 8:11). "Our Lord Jesus Christ . . . only hath immortality" (1 Tim. 6:14-16).

Those who teach the false soul-sleep theory delight in telling the public that we who hold to the true orthodox doctrine of life and consciousness after death, believe that man is now immortal. But such is not the case. We believe that man is now only mortal, just as the Scriptures state. The true orthodox teaching, according to the Scripture, is that man's soul is immortal, and that his body is mortal.

To recapitulate:

1. The resurrection body will be incorruptible and immortal. "It is sown in corruption, it is raised in incorruption" (1 Cor. 15:42). "For this corruptible must put on incorruption, and this mortal must put on immortality" (1 Cor. 15:53).

2. Paul continues to reveal the character of the resurrection body: "It [the body] is sown in dishonour; it is raised in glory" (1 Cor. 15:43). A body of dishonor no doubt means a body limited to the physical sphere—perhaps a disfigured or deformed body. There will be no more of this in the resurrection. The body is to be raised

"in glory," with no more physical limitations, and no more dishonor or shame.

3. Paul next declares that the body "is sown in weakness; it is raised in power" (1 Cor. 15:43). A dead body is a perfect example of weakness, yet God says of His redeemed children, He will raise the body with power.

4. "It is sown a natural body; it is raised a spiritual body" (1 Cor. 15:44). The use of the word "spiritual" in connection with the body does not mean that the resurrection body will be one that has no substance, as we shall soon see.

Thus far we have learned that the resurrection body will be incorruptible, immortal, glorious, powerful, and spiritual. But perhaps the most wonderful fact is yet to be considered. It floods the Christian with joy and hope.

5. The resurrection body of the believer will be like the resurrected, glorified body of Christ. The Scripture declares that the believer's resurrection body will be like that of our Saviour. Paul writes that Christ "shall change our vile body, that it may be fashioned like unto his glorious body" (Phil. 3:21). John adds, "We know that when he shall appear, we shall be like him; for we shall see him as he is" (1 John 3:2). The Psalmist sings, "As for me, I will behold thy face in righteousness: I shall be satisfied, when I awake, with thy likeness" (Ps. 17:15). We join him in his glad song.

What was Christ's resurrection body like?

It was a real body of visible shape and form. It was capable of being handled, yet was not restricted by physical walls and doors. Of the 10 appearances of Christ in His glorified body after the Resurrection, here are the records of 3. They show that Christ's body was a real body capable of being handled. Matthew tells us that the disciples "came and held him by the feet, and worshipped him" (Matt. 28:9).

When Christ appeared to the Eleven, He said, "Behold my hands and my feet, that it is I myself: handle me, and see; for a spirit hath not flesh and bones, as ye see me have" (Luke 24:39). John tells us that eight days later, when the doors of the room were shut, Jesus came and stood in the midst, and said to Thomas, "Reach hither thy finger, and behold my hands; and reach hither thy hand, and thrust it into my side" (John 20:27).

Christ's resurrection body was not only capable of being handled, and able to pass through materials, but it was also recognizable. Mary recognized Him in the Garden (John 20:16), and so did Mary Magdalene (John 20:18). The disciples recognized Him on the evening of the Resurrection Day (John 20:20). The believer's resurrection body will be a glorified body like Christ's—a real body that others will readily recognize.

6. There is yet another important fact to be considered. The resurrected, glorified body will not be a body of flesh and blood, because the Bible says that "flesh and blood cannot inherit the kingdom of God" (1 Cor. 15:50). The resurrection body will have no mortal flesh, and there will be no need for blood. Where there are no wasting body cells, there is no need of blood to supply nourishment to them.

We read that in heaven there shall be "neither hunger nor thirst," and there shall be no more sickness or death, and "there shall be no night there." Since none of these is going to have any place in heaven, it is easily seen that there will be no wasting of the body.

7. A body that will not waste away—one that is incorruptible, and immortal—will be eternal. This agrees with Luke 20:36, where Jesus says, "Neither can they die

any more"; and also with Rev. 22:5, which points out that the redeemed "shall reign for ever and ever."

From our study we have learned that the resurrection body will be incorruptible, immortal, glorious, powerful, spiritual—it will be like Christ's glorious body. It will be a body not of flesh and blood, but a body that shall endure eternally.

The discussion thus far has been about the resurrection body of the righteous dead, the "dead in Christ." What about the living believers, who shall be caught up together with the resurrection saints to meet the Lord in the air?

In 1 Cor. 15:51-52 Paul makes it clear that "we shall not all sleep, but we shall all be changed, in a moment, in the twinkling of an eye, at the last trump: for the trumpet shall sound, and the dead shall be raised incorruptible, and we shall be changed." We shall all be changed—the righteous who are "alive and remain," as well as "the dead in Christ." The next verse tells what the change will be. "This corruptible must put on incorruption, and this mortal must put on immortality." The change then for the living believer is a change from being subject to death to becoming free from death. It is logical and reasonable that the changed body of the living believer will have all the other glorious attributes that are characteristic of an incorruptible resurrection body.

We may add that such glorified bodies will not be bound to any specific place but may roam the universe at will. Also scientists now believe that light and time may be geared to the same speed. If this be true, when time ceases in eternity and there is only the light of God shining everywhere throughout the universe, there can be no such thing as age. The eternal absence of time and age means the limitless and endless enjoyment of paradise, without the possibility of aging or change.

# CHAPTER 11

# The Bliss of the Righteous

We have seen that the righteous are in the third heaven with Christ in their preglorified state. At Christ's coming, they will be glorified with resurrection bodies, and then be ready for entrance upon their eternal bliss. This glorification with resurrection bodies is what fits them for the habitation of the eternal heaven with God and the angels. This will constitute complete redemption for spirit, soul, and body; it will prepare the saints for eternity with God and Christ, the Saviour and Lord (see 1 Thess. 4:17).

Now let us look for a few moments to that heaven which the saints will inherit after they are totally ready for it. No saint has yet entered into the final heaven, just as no sinner has yet gone into the final hell. These are reserved for the saints and the sinners in their final states, after all things earthly have been consummated.

As indicated earlier, we must distinguish between the present heaven and the eternal heaven. The description of heaven from the fourth chapter of Revelation to the end of the book is future only. The description in the 21st chapter of the city of precious stones, pearly gates, and streets of gold is not a description of the present abode of believers who have died. All these chapters are future; every description applies to the eternal habitation of the believers. They cannot be used to describe the present heaven.

Here are references to the final heaven. It is spoken of as "a city which hath foundations, whose builder and maker is God." In Heb. 11:16 we read, "He hath prepared for them a city." Again in 13:14 we are told, "Here have we no continuing city, but we seek one to come." The city is described in Revelation 21. It is the New Jerusalem, or city foursquare. This city in itself is not the entire heaven; it is but a city of heaven. John tells us that he saw it "coming down from God out of heaven" (Rev. 21:2). This heavenly city is a prepared place for a prepared people. It is the place of which Jesus spoke, "I go to prepare a place for you . . . that where I am, there ye may be also" (John 14:2-3).

Heaven is also spoken of as a country. The author of Hebrews writes, "They seek a country." The ASV describes it as "a country of their own" (Heb. 11:14). In 11:16, we are told, "They desire a better country, that is, an heavenly."

Peter refers to heaven as a place where believers have an inheritance awaiting them (1 Pet. 1:3-5). So wonderful is this inheritance that Paul exclaims, "Eye hath not seen, nor ear heard, neither have entered into the heart of man, the things which God hath prepared for them that love him" (1 Cor. 2:9). Therefore he exhorts us, "Set your affection on things above, not on things on the earth" (Col. 3:2). In Matt. 6:20 Jesus admonishes us to lay up for ourselves treasures in heaven.

In Rev. 21:1-5 we find a description of the heavenly Jerusalem: "And I saw a new heaven and a new earth: for the first heaven and the first earth were passed away; and there was no more sea. And I John saw the holy city, new Jerusalem, coming down from God out of heaven, prepared as a bride adorned for her husband. And I heard a great voice out of heaven saying, Behold, the tabernacle of God is with men, and he will dwell with them, and they shall be his people, and God himself shall be with them, and be their God. And God shall wipe away all tears from their eyes; and there shall be no more death, neither sorrow, nor crying, neither shall there be any more pain: for the former things are passed away. And he that sat upon the throne said, Behold, I make all things new."

In Rev. 21:10, John says he saw the "holy Jerusalem." In her he saw (v. 11) "the glory of God: and her light was like unto a stone most precious, even like a jasper stone, clear as crystal." In verses 18-19 he adds, "The building of the wall of it was of jasper: and the city was pure gold, like unto clear glass. And the foundations of the wall of the city were garnished with all manner of precious stones." In verses 21-23 the vision continues: "The twelve gates were twelve pearls; every several gate was of one pearl. . . . And I saw no temple therein: for the Lord God Almighty and the Lamb are the temple of it. And the city had no need of the sun, neither of the moon, to shine in it: for the glory of God did lighten it, and the Lamb is the light thereof."

In verse 27 John describes the holiness of the city: "There shall in no wise enter into it any thing that defileth, neither whatsoever worketh abomination, or maketh a lie: but they which are written in the Lamb's book of life." In 22:3-5, the wonders continue: "There shall be no more curse: but the throne of God and of the Lamb shall be in it; and his servants shall serve him: and they shall see his face; and his name shall be in their foreheads. And there shall be no night there; and they need no candle, neither light of the sun; for the Lord God giveth them light: and they shall reign for ever and ever."

Heaven will have many marvels, but it will not be the pearly gates, or the jasper walls, or the streets of transparent gold, that will make it heaven. These would not satisfy us. If this were all, we would not want to stay there forever. It will be our association with God that will make heaven attractive. All the joys that we will know will come from the presence of God. The earthly beauties are used to try to convey heavenly beauties to our human minds. This is the only way that we are able to grasp, even in part, the beauties of heaven. Paul declares, "Eye hath not seen, nor ear heard, neither have entered into the heart of man, the things which God hath prepared for them that love him" (1 Cor. 2:9).

As we saw in Chapter 7, the Bible makes it clear that those in the present paradise recognize one another. It is only reasonable, then, that the righteous will also recognize one another in the final heaven.

In Matt. 8:11, Christ says, "I say unto you, That many shall come from the east and west, and shall sit down with Abraham, and Isaac, and Jacob, in the kingdom of heaven." These men lived hundreds of years before Christ, yet when the time comes when many shall come from the east and west and sit down with them in the final heaven, they will not have lost their identity. They will be known as Abraham, Isaac, and Jacob.

Christ was recognized after receiving His resurrection body. Mary Magdalene and the disciples recognized Him (John 20:16, 18, 20). On one occasion He appeared to 500. Since the believers' resurrection bodies are to have attributes like Christ's resurrection body, they will be recognizable.

As a closing note on the final abode of the righteous, consider the following:

It has been stated that the New Jerusalem, as a perfect cube described in Revelation, would be about 1,500 miles in every direction—height, breadth, and length. Suppose this city were divided into one half for the throne of God and the courts of the angels. The other half could be assigned for the "mansions" that Jesus mentioned (John 14:1). Mathematicians have calculated that in this half there would in terms of earthly measurement, be room enough for all the people from 100 worlds like this to have a personal mansion of 100 rooms, each room 16 feet square. There will be plenty of room for all the inhabitants in that grand land.

Since glorified bodies will not necessarily be restricted to any one area, we may roam the universe at will. Just as each country has a capital city, so apparently the New Jerusalem will be the capital of the universe.

We now know that the universe of sidereal space is at least 1 billion light-years across. Light moving at 186,000 miles per second would travel about 6 trillion miles in an ordinary year. This 6 trillion miles is known to astronomers as a light-year. Six trillion times 1 billion gives the approximate mileage astronomers have calculated as the distance across the known universe. It may be farther, for no one knows yet the vastness of sidereal space.

Arcturus, one of the larger stars, is said to be 428 million miles in diameter. The Andromeda galaxy, in our own system of the Milky Way, is 700,000 light-years away, and 60,000 light-years across. But this is small compared to the greatest star so far discovered. Alpha Herculis reports in as 2.4 billion miles in diameter. There are now known to be more than 21 trillion stars scintillating in our heavens.

Over this vast universe the saints of God may roam at will forever. In fact, it belongs to us, for the Bible says, "All things are yours" (1 Cor. 3:21). And Paul adds that we are "heirs of God, and joint-heirs with Christ" (Rom.

8:17). All that the Heavenly Father possesses, we will also possess as His heirs in that illimitable vastness of the universe. We will be at home anywhere in that great domain. It may be basking in the light of the New Jerusalem, or enjoying a reception for angels or for earthly friends in some indescribably beautiful mansion, or roaming over the surface of some huge star at the end of the universe.

# The Prison House of the Damned

Hell is not a pleasant subject and the doctrine of hell is not a popular doctrine. But it is one that we should understand and face up to, especially those who are in danger of going there.

Sinners sometimes make a mock of being lost, and reject the doctrine of eternal punishment. One writer tells us that "few educated people at the present day trouble their heads about everlasting damnation or fires of hell; the old doctrine of hell is dying. It was something for the medieval ages." This position, sadly enough, lacks confirmation in the Bible.

The first argument usually advanced against hell is that a God of love couldn't send anyone there. We hear that "God is too good, He is too just to send men to hell." We agree that God sends no one to hell. Rather, men condemn themselves to eternal punishment by rejecting Christ as their personal Saviour and by neglecting God's plan of salvation.

It may be true that the attitude of people toward the doctrine of hell has changed, but the Word of God is unchangeable. Our ideas will not alter or change the truth. Hell is a place as truly as heaven is a place. The only way we can silence the awful truth of hell is by sealing the lips of the Son of God.

The Bible speaks of the wrath of God more frequently (61 times) than it does of His love (28 times). Not because God's wrath is greater than His mercy, but because it is His purpose to warn men of the punishment for sin. It is remarkable that both Jesus and John, who more than any others in the New Testament represent the love of God, speak most of the punishment of the wicked.

In preceding chapters we have distinguished between the present heaven (paradise) and the future heaven (New Jerusalem). We must now distinguish between the present hell and the hell of the future. The Bible is clear on this point, but for a proper understanding of the scriptural teaching we must turn to the original Greek. The Greek words *hades, gehenna,* and *tartarus* have all been translated into English in the King James Version by the one word "hell." In Luke 16:22-23, Christ said, "The rich man also died, and was buried; and in hell *[hades]* he lift up his eyes." In Matt. 23:33 our Lord said, "Ye serpents, ye generation of vipers, how can ye escape the damnation of hell *[gehenna]?*" In 2 Pet. 2:4 we read, "God spared not the angels that sinned, but cast them down to hell *[tartarus].*"

From reading the King James Version, in which the three different words are translated "hell," it is impossible for the reader to recognize there are three different places. As a result, many people have been confused and have not clearly distinguished the present hell from the place of future punishment.


### The Present Abode of the Wicked

Just as there is a present paradise for the righteous to occupy until they received their resurrection bodies, and a final heaven for them, so there is a present abode for the unrighteous, and a final hell for them.

The Bible clearly distinguishes between the present abode and the future place for the departed spirits of the wicked. In Luke 16:19-31, Christ made it clear that the place of torment in *hades* is the present abode of the unrighteous. The final hell is distinguished from the present abode of the wicked by the use of a different word, *gehenna*. This is the word used by Christ for the final hell.

The Greek word, *tartarus*, is found only in 2 Pet. 2:4. The term does not refer to the abode of any departed human spirits; rather, it is the prison of fallen angels. Peter tells us, "God spared not the angels that sinned, but cast them down to hell *[tartarus]*, and delivered them into chains of darkness, to be reserved unto judgment" (2 Pet. 2:4). Jude gives a supporting clue: "The angels which kept not their first estate, but left their own habitation, he hath reserved in everlasting chains under darkness unto the judgment of the great day" (Jude 6).

The place in which the fallen angels are confined is clearly distinguished from the present abode of the wicked. The hell in which the fallen angels are confined is *tartarus;* and the present hell, the abode of unrighteous human spirits, is *hades.*

As previously stated, in Old Testament days, and in the days of the earthly ministry of Christ, the spirits of all the dead departed to *sheol* (Hebrew) or *hades* (Greek). Since the resurrection of our Lord, the righteous are no longer in the section they once occupied in *hades;* they are now in paradise, in the third heaven, in the presence of Christ. Since the resurrection and ascension of Christ the section for the righteous in *hades* has not been occupied.

The abode for the unrighteous dead, however, has not been changed. All the unrighteous who die depart to *hades* into the place of torment, just as they did before the resurrection and ascension of Christ.

The proof that this place in *hades* will be the abode of the unrighteous until they are resurrected for the final judgment is found in Rev. 20:13, which speaks of the resurrection and judgment of the wicked. "Death [the grave] and hell *[hades]* delivered up the dead which were in them: and they were judged every man according to their works."

Here we see that at the time of the resurrection and judgment of the wicked, *hades* is still the abode of the unrighteous. Luke 16:22-23 shows that *hades* was the abode of the wicked dead in the time of Christ; Rev. 20:13 indicates that it still is at the time the wicked are to be raised and judged.

In His story of the rich man and Lazarus (Luke 16:19-31), Jesus made clear that in *hades* the rich man's spirit was alive and conscious—he could see because he recognized Abraham and Lazarus, he could feel, thirst, talk, and remember. Five times Jesus said he was "in torment." A scripture that is as strong and unmistakable in meaning as this is fatal to doctrines which teach that the dead are unconscious and that there is no hell.

Of course, the Jehovah's Witnesses and others who believe and teach that the dead are unconscious and that there is no hell, try to explain away the truth of this passage. According to Rutherford's interpretation, the rich man is supposed to represent the nation of Israel, and Lazarus represents all the Gentile nations. "The drop of water in the parable pictures the small measure of truth that would help refresh the Israelites in their distress." Bible expositors do not accept such an interpretation. The inescapable truth is that after death the unrighteous are punished in hell; they are alive and conscious; they are able to see, hear, talk, feel, remember, and recognize each other.

### The Resurrection of the Wicked

Just as the righteous will not remain in paradise to spend eternity in a disembodied state, so the unrighteous will not remain in the present *hades* to spend eternity as disembodied spirits; they will receive resurrected bodies and spend eternity in the final hell.

It seems clear that the resurrection referred to in Rev. 20:13 is the resurrection of the wicked. The scripture says that *hades* "delivered up the dead." Only the spirits of the wicked are now confined in *hades;* the righteous are with Christ in the heavenlies. Furthermore, Rev. 20:5 says that after the first resurrection (resurrection of the righteous) "the rest of the dead lived not again until the thousand years were finished." Since the first resurrection is the resurrection of the righteous, then the rest of the dead must necessarily be the wicked. The resurrection of the wicked will occur 1,000 years after the resurrection of the righteous, that is, 1,000 years after the second coming of Christ. (This 1,000 years is known as the millennium period.)

At this resurrection, according to Rev. 20:13 the grave will deliver up the bodies, and *hades* will deliver up the spirits of the wicked. Thus the unrighteous will again be united with their bodies.

The Scripture is strangely silent about what the resurrection bodies of the wicked will be like. However, we are sure that the bodies of the wicked will not be like the believers' immortal, glorified bodies. God would not give the wonderful attributes of a glorified body to those who are to spend eternity in hell.

In speaking of the resurrection bodies, Paul said, "to every seed his own body" (1 Cor. 15:38). In this connection we recall the familiar scripture, "Whatsoever a man soweth, that shall he also reap." We know that a man cannot sow tares and expect to reap wheat; we reap exactly what we sow. Those who die without the Christ-life cannot rise to a Christ-life resurrection. The dead will be resurrected the same-in-kind as they were buried.

## The Great White Throne Judgment

After the unrighteous receive their resurrected bodies, they will appear at the great white throne judgment. Peter speaks of this as "the day of judgment and perdition of ungodly men" (2 Pet. 3:7). John adds, "Death and hell delivered up the dead which were in them: and they were judged every man according to their works" (Rev. 20:13). Verse 11 speaks of the great white throne, therefore we call it the great white throne judgment. The wicked will stand before God, and the books will be opened. They will be judged from these books according to their works. But also "another book" will be opened; it is the "book of life" in which will appear the names of those who are saved (Luke 10:20; Phil. 4:3; Heb. 12:23; Rev. 21:27).

No doubt many of the unrighteous will be found to have been respectable citizens and perhaps even liberal contributors to the church. But regardless of the record, whether good or bad, if their names are not found in the book of life they are "cast into the lake of fire" (Rev. 20:15). If their names do not appear there it will be because they rejected Christ as their Saviour and neglected God's plan of salvation. The supreme question in that day will be "Is your name in the book of life?"

The wicked will be judged not to see whether they are entitled to eternal life, but to determine their degree of punishment. The record of works, as found in the first books, will determine this punishment.

We read that after sinners have appeared at the great white throne judgment, "Death and hell were cast into the lake of fire [final hell]. . . . And whosoever was not found written in the book of life was cast into the lake of fire" (Rev. 20:14-15). We are told further that the "unbelieving . . . shall have their part in the lake which burneth with fire and brimstone" (Rev. 21:8). The sentence includes all the wicked; we do not read that any escape. This is called "the second death" (Rev. 20:14; 21:8).

The second death does not mean unconsciousness, nonexistence, or annihilation, any more than the first death does. In the second death, it may be that the wicked will lose their bodies a second time and again become disembodied spirits to exist in the lake of fire forever. This view is in harmony with what has already been said, namely that the bodies of the wicked will not be immortal, and therefore will be subject to death.

The Jehovah's Witnesses tell us that men will be given a second chance for salvation. But the Bible teaches no such doctrine. If the ungodly are to have a second chance for salvation after death, surely God made a great mistake when, at such great pains, He ordained that the Bible, the preaching of the gospel, and the striving of the Holy Spirit should lead men to Christ and salvation in this life. If there is a second chance, these would appear to be unnecessary.

Surely there can be no mistake in holding that the wicked are currently in conscious torment. The present hell is truly God's prison house of the damned. He has nowhere else to place people who deliberately choose to follow the devil in this life and come to the close of life in his service. There must be some provision for detaining their spirits until the final judgment; and this seems to have been God's best method for doing it.

# CHAPTER 13

# Is There Everlasting Punishment?

In opening this discussion, perhaps it is well to look again at some of the words used with reference to eternal punishment. It is clear from the account in Revelation 20—21 that the lake of fire and brimstone will be the final abode of Satan, the fallen angels, and the wicked people of the earth.

At the present time, the final hell of the universe (*gehenna,* the lake of fire) is not occupied. The first ones to be cast into it will be the "beast" and the "false prophet" (Rev. 19:20). Satan and his angels will be sent there 1,000 years later (Rev. 20:10). Finally, after the great white throne judgment, all the wicked who will be delivered up from *hades* to be judged will be cast into the lake of fire to spend eternity (Rev. 20:12-15).

The word used by Christ for the final hell was *gehenna,* not *hades.* This Greek word occurs in the New Testament 12 times. Five times the words "lake of fire" are used to describe it. The term comes from the Hebrew *Ghi-Hinnom* or "Valley of Hinnom." In the Old Testament this place is called Tophet (2 Kings 23:10; Isa. 30:33; Jer. 7:31-32; 19:6). It was on the south side of the city of Jerusalem. In the valley there was a certain promontory called "Tophet," and during the times of Isaiah and Jeremiah, numbers of backslidden Jews here forced their children to pass through the fire in worship of the false god Molech (2 Kings 23:10). According to Isa. 30:33, this fire was kindled with brimstone. The valley afterward became a place for burning the garbage of the city of Jerusalem. The refuse of the city was thrown over the wall into the valley below where the fires were kept burning continually. Some of the decaying garbage would lodge on the rocks of the wall and breed worms. Jesus used this valley as a figure of hell, the lake of fire. Therefore we read in Mark 9:43-44, "Where their worm dieth not, and the fire is not quenched."

In the following passages Christ used the Greek word *gehenna* for "hell" in its final sense:

"I say unto you, That whosoever is angry with his brother without a cause shall be in danger of the judgment: and whosoever shall say to his brother, Raca, shall be in danger of the council: but whosoever shall say, Thou fool, shall be in danger of hell fire" (Matt. 5:22).

"If thy right eye offend thee, pluck it out, and cast it from thee: for it is profitable for thee that one of thy members should perish, and not that thy whole body should be cast into hell" (Matt. 5:29-30; see also 18:9).

"Fear not them which kill the body, but are not able to kill the soul: but rather fear him which is able to destroy both soul and body in hell" (Matt. 10:28).

"Woe unto you, scribes and Pharisees, hypocrites! for ye compass sea and land to make one proselyte, and when he is made, ye make him twofold more the child of hell than yourselves" (Matt. 23:15).

"Ye serpents, ye generation of vipers, how can ye escape the damnation of hell?" (Matt. 23:33).

"If thy hand offend thee, cut it off: it is better for thee to enter into life maimed, than having two hands to go into hell, into the fire that never shall be quenched" (Mark 9:43).

"I will forewarn you whom ye shall fear: Fear him, which after he hath killed hath power to cast into hell; yea, I say unto you, Fear him" (Luke 12:5).

These passages are clearly distinguished from the ones which use the word *hades* for the present hell.

The Bible describes this final hell as a place of fire. Note these passages:

Matt. 3:12, "He will burn up the chaff with unquenchable fire."

Matt. 5:22, "Whosoever shall say, Thou fool, shall be in danger of hell fire."

Matt. 13:41-42, "Them which do iniquity; and shall cast them into a furnace of fire: there shall be wailing and gnashing of teeth."

Matt. 18:8, "To be cast into everlasting fire."

Matt. 18:9, "To be cast into hell fire."

Matt. 25:41, "Depart from me, ye cursed, into everlasting fire."

Mark 9:43, 45, "The fire that never shall be quenched."

Mark 9:44, 46, 48, "Where their worm dieth not, and the fire is not quenched."

Rev. 20:15, "Whosoever was not found written in the book of life was cast into the lake of fire."

Rev. 21:8, "The fearful, and unbelieving, and the abominable, and murderers, and whoremongers, and sorcerers, and idolaters, and all liars, shall have their part in the lake which burneth with fire and brimstone: which is the second death."

The question in most people's minds seems to be, Is this "hell fire" a literal flame or is it symbolic of a severe punishment?

In view of the frequent symbolic use of the word "fire"

elsewhere in the Bible, it would seem that the references to "hell fire" are also symbolic of the intense agony and suffering of hell.

Let us study the following passages carefully.

Ps. 78:21, "Therefore the Lord heard this, and was wroth: so a fire was kindled against Jacob, and anger also came up against Israel."

Ps. 104:4, "Who maketh his angels spirits; his ministers a flaming fire."

1 Cor. 3:13, "Every man's work shall be made manifest: for the day shall declare it, because it shall be revealed by fire; and the fire shall try every man's work of what sort it is."

Heb. 12:29, "Our God is a consuming fire."

Jas. 3:6, "The tongue is a fire, a world of iniquity: so is the tongue among our members, that it defileth the whole body, and setteth on fire the course of nature; and it is set on fire of hell."

1 Pet. 1:7, "That the trial of your faith, being much more precious than of gold that perisheth, though it be tried with fire, might be found unto praise and honour and glory at the appearing of Jesus Christ."

See also Ps. 66:10-12; Jer. 23:29; Zech. 13:9.

Would it seem from these uses that a literal flame was meant? If not, is it not reasonable to suppose that the fire of hell is not meant to be a literal flame of fire but rather symbolic?

Let it be clearly understood, however, that just because it is believed that this word "fire" is symbolic, we are not trying to show that the punishment of hell will be less severe than it would be if there were literal flames. On the contrary, if this fire is symbolic, then the punishment will be all the greater because the reality is always greater than the symbol. Whether the fire spoken of is literal or figurative, the fact remains that there is severe eternal punishment in hell.

The condition of the lost is described in other terms as well, such as "cast out into outer darkness: there shall be weeping and gnashing of teeth." The terms "weeping and gnashing of teeth" are found together seven times (Matt. 8:12; 13:42, 50; 22:13; 24:51; 25:30; Luke 13:28).

For anyone to say that there is no future punishment in hell for the wicked is to ignore scores of plain statements in the Bible. And according to the biblical description of that place, neither can anyone deny the dreadfulness and severity of the punishment.

### Theories Concerning Final Destiny

1. *Annihilation Theory.* Of the various false theories concerning the final destiny of the wicked, one of the most often heard of is the annihilation theory. The word *annihilate* means to reduce to nothing, to wipe out of existence. Those who believe this theory believe that when they die, or after the final judgment, the wicked will simply cease to exist.

There are many forms of this theory. Some teach that the wicked are annihilated at death, never to be brought back into existence. Then there are those, like Rutherford, who teach that the wicked are annihilated at death, but that they will all be recreated and restored to consciousness in order to be given a second chance for salvation. This "bringing back into existence and restoring to consciousness" is called "resurrection."

The Jehovah's Witnesses teach that after the wicked have been "recreated" they will be given a trial for life, as a second chance, or as Russell says, "an opportunity to gain everlasting life, under favorable terms." This is what Russell calls "the judgment." And according to the theory, those who refuse the second chance for eternal life will be cast into the lake of fire and will be annihilated—that is, consciousness and existence will both end; the wicked will cease to exist. The Bible gives no support for such a doctrine.

The first part of this theory has already been refuted, for the Bible teaches that after death the soul is conscious, and the Bible nowhere teaches a second chance.

Now let us examine proof from the Bible that the annihilationists are wrong when they say that the wicked will cease to exist when they are cast into the lake of fire. These false teachers try to prove their position by saying that words such as "destroy," "destruction," "perish," and "consume" mean annihilation.

For example, they say that 2 Thess. 1:9 means annihilation: "who shall be punished with everlasting destruction." This is supposed to teach that the wicked will be put out of existence. Likewise, the word "destroyed" is also claimed to teach that the wicked will be annihilated. And because several passages infer that the wicked are to "perish" and are to be "consumed," it is argued that they must therefore go out of existence. But such an interpretation is not correct.

Here is a test which shows that these words do not necessarily mean annihilation. In the following references the words *annihilate* or *annihilation* are substituted for the words "destroyed" or "destruction."

Ps. 78:45, "He sent . . . frogs, which destroyed [annihilated] them." If the word "destroyed" meant annihilation, the frogs have been endowed with the power to put the Egyptians out of existence.

Job 19:10, "He hath destroyed [annihilated] me on every side." Again, if the word meant annihilation, Job was put out of existence, yet he lived to tell about it.

Job 21:17, "How oft cometh their destruction [annihilation] upon them." How could they be put out of existence many times?

Isa. 34:2, "For the indignation of the Lord is upon all nations . . . he hath utterly destroyed [annihilated] them." Here again, if the word "destroyed" meant annihilation, the nations were put out of existence, yet they are still here.

Jer. 17:18, "Destroy [annihilate] them with double destruction [annihilation]." They were to be doubly put out of existence.

Heb. 2:14 says that Christ came to destroy the devil. But did Christ "annihilate" him? Did He put him out of existence? No! The devil is still in existence, and from Rev. 20:10, we see that he will be in existence for ever and ever.

If the words "destroy" and "destruction" in these instances cannot be forced to mean annihilation, they need not mean annihilation when applied to everlasting punishment of the wicked.

Some argue for annihilation from 2 Thess. 1:9: "Who shall be punished with everlasting destruction from the presence of the Lord, and from the glory of his power." Those who teach annihilation say that no man can be put away from the presence of an omnipresent God without being put out of existence. But let us turn to Gen. 4:16, where we read that "Cain went out from the presence of the Lord." Nevertheless, according to the scripture, we find that he lived after this in the land of Nod and had a family. The Divine Presence is more powerfully and gloriously manifest in heaven than anywhere else, and it is from this presence that the unjust will be forever banished.

Let us now look at the use of the word "perish." Those who teach that the wicked will be annihilated after they are cast into the lake of fire, say that the word "perish" also signifies going out of existence.

The word for "perish" in the original Greek is *apollumi*. It denotes "ruin" or "rendering unfit for the intended use," not going out of existence. For example, in Matt. 9:17 we read, "The bottles break, and the wine runneth out, and the bottles perish." If the bottle (wineskin) is broken, it is only rendered unfit for its intended use; it has not been annihilated. In Mark's account this same word is translated "marred" instead of "perish."

In Luke 15:17, the prodigal son said, "I perish with hunger." Was he about to be annihilated?

In 2 Pet. 3:6 we read, "The world . . . being overflowed with water, perished." But was the earth reduced to nothing? From all indications it is still here.

Of the heavens and earth it is said, "They shall perish" (Heb. 1:11). Yet when this perishing is explained, it is said, "They shall be changed."

In Matt. 10:6, this same word *apollumi* is translated "lost" instead of "perish" (cf. Matt. 15:24). Jesus said, "Go rather to the lost sheep." If the sheep were annihilated, how could anyone go to them? Also in Luke 15:24 the prodigal son is said to be "lost," yet he was not out of existence.

Now let us look at the word "consume." In the following test, try substituting the word *annihilate* for the word "consume" or their counterparts.

David said, "I shall now perish ['be consumed,' margin] one day by the hand of Saul" (1 Sam. 27:1). Surely David did not expect Saul to annihilate him.

The Psalmist said, "Mine eye is consumed" (Ps. 6:7), and "My bones are consumed" (Ps. 31:10). And yet neither his eye nor his bones were put out of existence.

God said of the children of Israel, "I have consumed them in mine anger" (Ezek. 43:8), yet they were then living by the hundreds of thousands.

"Take heed," says the apostle, "that ye be not consumed one of another" (Gal. 5:15). Were they to take heed that they should not annihilate one another?

The Antichrist, "whom the Lord shall consume with the spirit of his mouth, and shall destroy with the brightness of his coming" (2 Thess. 2:8), will not be annihilated; we find him 1,000 years later in the lake of fire and brimstone (Rev. 20:10).

Again, the teachers of this annihilation theory tell us that the words "burned up" used in reference to the wicked must mean that they will be put out of existence.

Mal. 4:1 says, "For, behold, the day cometh, that shall burn as an oven; and all the proud, yea, and all that do wickedly, shall be stubble: and the day that cometh shall burn them up, saith the Lord of hosts, that it shall leave them neither root nor branch."

In the first place it may be said that a literal burning cannot annihilate anything. A building may be destroyed by fire; but, as science clearly teaches, no particle of the matter is annihilated. Wood may be placed in the fire, and by the process of combustion it may be decomposed. Its elements are scattered in the form of flame, and vapor, and smoke, and ashes, but nothing goes out of existence. Things pass from one form into another but are not reduced to nothingness. There is no annihilation of anything material; there are only changes of form.

In our discussion at the beginning of the chapter, it was said that the fire was probably a symbol of the terrible reality of the suffering of hell, rather than a literal flame. In this view, the burning up here referred to would symbolize a severe and dreadful punishment.

To summarize, the words "destroy," "destruction," and "perish" do not mean annihilation. They simply denote "to ruin" or "to render unfit for the intended use," or "to change the form of existence."

Furthermore, the annihilation theory contradicts the Bible teaching that there are degrees of reward and punishment. In Rom. 2:6, we are told that God "will render to every man according to his deeds." In Rev. 20:13 it says that "they were judged every man according to their works." But if the wicked are put out of existence, they will be punished every man alike.

2. *The Restoration Theory.* Another of the false theories concerning the final destiny of the wicked is that of restoration. This theory teaches that after the wicked have been punished in the *gehenna* of fire a sufficient length of time for their sins, and after they have been purified, they will be brought out and transferred to heaven. Those who believe in this theory use several passages which, they claim, teach that the wicked will be finally reconciled to God.

Acts 3:20-21, "Jesus Christ . . . whom the heaven must receive until the times of restitution of all things, which God hath spoken by the mouth of all his holy prophets since the world began."

Those who teach the restoration theory claim that "all things" includes Satan, his angels, and all the wicked, and that at a time of restitution they will be restored and reconciled to God. But carefully examine the text. The next clause says that the restoration is to be only of all things "which God hath spoken by the mouth of all his holy prophets." Nowhere in the Bible has God spoken "by the mouth of his holy prophets" that He would restore the wicked or Satan and his angels to everlasting righteousness after they have been punished for a certain length of time. Rather, Rev. 20:10 says that the punishment will be for ever and ever.

It is also plain that this restoration refers to those who have been reconciled to God through Christ. From 2 Cor. 5:18 we read, "God, who hath reconciled us [Christians] to himself by Jesus Christ." In Col. 1:20-21, those who are reconciled were at one time aliens and enemies by wicked words, but now they have made their peace through the blood of His cross. This reconcilation to God is not a hope to be realized by the lost in hell. Rather is is for all who have been reconciled to God through Christ in this present life.

Those who believe in the restoration theory also use Phil. 2:10-11 to attempt to show that the wicked will be restored to heaven: "At the name of Jesus every knee should bow, of things in heaven, and things in earth, and things under the earth; and that every tongue should confess that Jesus Christ is Lord."

The fact that all will confess Christ as Lord does not imply that the lost, who are compelled to admit it, will be taken to heaven. For the lost to confess that Christ is Lord does not mean that they will have a change of heart. Repentance and faith in Christ are necessary to keep out of hell. The Bible says, "Except ye repent, ye shall all likewise perish" (Luke 13:3). God commandeth all men everywhere to repent. It is repentance that leads to a change of heart and salvation. According to the examples from the Bible, a period of suffering does not always cause repentance. In instances where suffering has been inflicted upon the wicked, the punishment has sometimes hardened the wicked, instead of causing them to repent.

In the Book of Revelation we are told that the wicked who suffered from the plagues, instead of repenting and calling on God, cried for the rocks and mountains to fall on them and hide them from God (Rev. 6:16). When the plague of hail came, instead of repenting, they blasphemed God (Rev. 16:21). Even Satan, after suffering 1,000 years in the bottomless pit, comes out as wicked as ever (Rev. 20:7-8).

The fact that the lost as well as Satan will confess

that Christ is Lord does not mean that they will be taken to heaven. The Bible plainly shows that Satan is to be tormented in the lake of fire for ever and ever (Rev. 20:10). We understand that the fate of the lost will be the same. According to the Bible, after the wicked have been cast into the lake of fire, they will neither be annihilated nor later restored to heaven.

### *Everlasting Punishment*

The final hell is a place of eternal duration just as is the final heaven. In a moral universe, there can be no eternal heaven without its counterpart, an eternal hell. The one demands the other. If the punishment of hell is not eternal, what was the purpose of Christ's supreme sacrifice on Calvary? Christ suffered and died on the Cross to bring men to God. Certainly He made too great a sacrifice if there is no eternal hell from which to save men. It is true, God is love—but God is also just. He must keep the righteous from the wicked. Thus it is necessary that they be separated for all eternity.

God has revealed the truth of eternal punishment and we cannot teach otherwise. Here are Christ's own words: "And these [the wicked] shall go away into everlasting punishment: but the righteous into life eternal" (Matt. 25:46).

Here the punishment of the wicked is said to be everlasting and the life of the righteous is eternal. Is there a difference? When we examine the original Greek, we find that these two words are the same. The one Greek word *aionios* is translated one time "everlasting" and the other time "eternal." Both may be correctly translated as "eternal." The punishment of the wicked will be just exactly as long as the life of the righteous.

Those who teach that the punishment of the wicked

will not be endless try to prove it by pointing out that the word *aionios* means only "agelong," or "for a period." It is true that this word comes from *aion,* which means age. But it is the only word in Greek that can be used to express the idea of "eternal" or "everlasting."

Sometimes the word means "agelong"; sometimes it means "eternal." Only by studying the context can we be sure which meaning was intended. In the cases where the word is used to mean an age or period that is to come to an end, the rest of the verse makes this clear (see Matt. 24:3; 28:20).

In the New Testament *aionios* is used 71 times, and in all but four places it is translated "eternal" or "everlasting." In these places no other meaning could suit the context. When *aionios* is applied to human destiny, the rest of the verse shows that it does not mean "agelong." For example, in 2 Cor. 4:18 Paul writes, "The things which are seen are temporal; but the things which are not seen are eternal *[aionios]*." Here the word is in sharp contrast to what is temporary or "for a period."

This is the very same word that we find in Rom. 16:26, "The commandment of the everlasting *[aionios]* God." If the word means endless duration when applied to the existence of God and when applied to the existence of the righteous, it also means endless duration when applied to the existence and punishment of the wicked.

In the Greek the expression "for ever and ever" is *eis tous aionas ton aionon.* It clearly means endless duration or eternity. This expression is used in speaking of the sinful followers of the Antichrist: "And the smoke of their torment ascendeth up for ever and ever: and they have no rest day nor night" (Rev. 14:11). The expression is also used to say that Satan "shall be tormented day and night for ever and ever" (Rev. 20:10). The glorified Christ testifies of himself, "I am he that liveth, and was dead; and, behold, I am alive for evermore" (Rev. 1:18).

This expression is also used of the existence of God; He is called the One "who liveth for ever and ever" (Rev. 4:9-10; 5:14; 10:6; 15:7). In Rev. 22:5 it is said of the righteous, "They shall reign for ever and ever."

How long will the life of the righteous be? The Bible says, "for ever and ever." Then the punishment of the wicked will also be "for ever and ever."

Jesus said solemnly, "And these [the wicked] shall go away into everlasting punishment" (Matt. 25:46). Paul writes, "Taking vengeance on them that know not God, and that obey not the gospel of our Lord Jesus Christ: who shall be punished with everlasting destruction" (2 Thess. 1:8-9). Daniel predicts of the dead, "Some [shall awake] to everlasting life, and some to shame and everlasting contempt" (Dan. 12:2).

Again Jesus said, "He that shall blaspheme against the Holy Ghost hath never forgiveness, but is in danger of eternal damnation" (Mark 3:29). And still further we read, "Depart from me, ye cursed, into everlasting fire, prepared for the devil and his angels" (Matt. 25:41). Of those who sin against God, He warns that they are in danger of being "cast into everlasting fire" (Matt. 18:8).

Speaking of evil men, Jude writes, "To whom is reserved the blackness of darkness for ever" (v. 13). The Psalmist warns the wicked, "God shall likewise destroy thee for ever" (Ps. 52:5); and, "When the wicked spring as the grass, and when all the workers of iniquity do flourish; it is that they shall be destroyed for ever" (Ps. 92:7).

Finally, speaking of the place of eternal punishment, Jesus declared "their worm dieth not, and the fire is not quenched" (Mark 9:44, 46, 48).

In speaking of this everlasting punishment, the annihilationists would say that the "everlasting" refers to the results or consequences of that punishment and not to the punishment itself. Banishment to hell is eternal punishment in the sense that the wicked will be eternally annihilated, not eternally suffering. But annihilation would be ended punishment rather than endless punishment. And besides, how can there be such a thing as unconscious punishment? A brick or a house cannot be punished. Punishment can take place only where there is consciousness.

It is a remarkable fact that the ministers and churches that have believed most firmly in the doctrine of eternal punishment have been the most influential in leading sinners to Christ.

And here is a note of interest in regard to the attitude of unbelievers toward the biblical doctrine of hell. Some who at one time denounced the Bible and its teaching concerning the punishment of the wicked, when faced with death, have expressed in their dying words their belief in hell.

Oh the insufferable pangs of hell. Oh eternity, forever and forever.—Newport

I would gladly give one hundred and fifty thousand dollars to have it proved that there is no hell.— Charteres

I would gladly give worlds, if I had them, if *The Age of Reason* had not been published. O Lord, help me. Christ, help me. Stay with me. It is hell to be left alone.—Tom Paine

Voltaire cried, "I am abandoned by God and man. O Christ, O Christ Jesus." He then said, "Doctor, I will give you half of what I am worth if you will give me six months of life." The doctor answered, "Sir, you cannot live six weeks." Voltaire replied, "Then I shall go to hell," and soon after expired.

Here is a truth that should set everyone to serious thinking. It is the plain teaching of the Bible that heaven is forever closed to those who die unsaved. Jesus himself said, "Except a man be born again, he cannot see the kingdom of God" (John 3:3).

Again Christ says, speaking of sinners who will die in their sins, "I go, my way, and ye shall seek me, and shall die in your sins: whither I go, ye cannot come" (John 8:21). If men die in their sins, they must be shut out of heaven forever, because they can never go where Jesus is. From our study of the rich man and Lazarus, we see that there are no conversions in the realm of the lost (Luke 16:19-31).

The climax to this solemn truth that heaven is forever closed to those who die unsaved is found in the words of the Apostle John. He declares concerning the dead, "He that is unjust, let him be unjust still: and he which is filthy, let him be filthy still: and he that is righteous, let him be righteous still" (Rev. 22:11). Death does not change character, it only petrifies it.

In summary, the Scriptures teach the eternal punishment of the wicked. There is no court of appeal from Holy Writ. It stands unalterable, with the weight of God's sovereign Being behind it.

# CHAPTER 14

# The Blessed Way of Escape

God has provided salvation for all men who will hear the gospel, believe its truth, and accept the Saviour. Through the centuries God has been calling men to repentance: "Come now, let us reason together, saith the Lord: though your sins be as scarlet, they shall be as white as snow; though they be red like crimson, they shall be as wool" (Isa. 1:18). And again, "Seek ye the Lord while he may be found, call ye upon him while he is near: let the wicked forsake his way, and the unrighteous man his thoughts: and let him return unto the Lord, and he will have mercy upon him; and to our God, for he will abundantly pardon" (Isa. 55:6-7).

We must face the issue squarely. Are we prepared to die? Where will we spend eternity? In heaven or in hell? Preparation can be made to give us the assurance of heaven. We can be ready to meet our Maker. God's way of salvation is so plain that no man need err therein. That way is marked in plain red—it is the way of Christ and His shed blood. Jesus said, "I am the way" (John 14:6).

According to the Bible, we are all accountable. Paul writes, "Every one of us shall give account of himself to God" (Rom. 14:12); "The scripture hath concluded all under sin" (Gal. 3:22); "All have sinned, and come short of the glory of God" (Rom. 3:23). Elsewhere in the Scriptures we read, "There is no man that sinneth not" (1 Kings 8:46); "If we say that we have no sin, we deceive ourselves, and the truth is not in us" (1 John 1:8); "If we say that we have not sinned, we make him [Christ] a liar" (1 John 1:10; cf. Rom. 5:12).

The Bible says that all are under sin, and that none can be saved by his own good works. Paul writes, "Not by works of righteousness which we have done, but according to his mercy he saved us" (Titus 3:5); "For by grace ye are saved through faith; and that not of yourselves: it is the gift of God: not of works, lest any man should boast" (Eph. 2:8-9). Our good works will not obtain salvation for us, because our righteousness is as filthy rags in His sight (Isa. 64:6).

Some depend for their salvation on church membership, on being respectable citizens, supporting their families, contributing to the poor or to the upkeep of the church. But such good works do not bring salvation. Salvation depends not upon our merit but upon personal acceptance of Jesus Christ. Jesus declared, "Except a man be born again, he cannot see the kingdom of God" (John 3:3).

1. *What it means to be born again.* Regeneration is not water baptism, or confirmation, neither is it reformation. Regeneration is not the old nature altered, reformed, or reinvigorated. It is not a reforming process on the part of man, and it is not a natural forward step in man's development. *Regeneration is a new birth from above.* It is a supernatural, creative act on the part of God. The sinner receives a new nature—God's nature—and he puts on the "new man" which God creates after holiness and righteousness.

"A new heart also will I give you, and a new spirit

will I put within you" (Ezek. 36:26). "If any man be in Christ, he is a new creature: old things are passed away; behold, all things are become new" (2 Cor. 5:17; cf. Eph. 4:24).

By regeneration we are admitted into the kingdom of God. There is no other way of becoming a Christian but by being born of the Spirit of God. As we enter this world by the process of natural birth, so we enter the kingdom of God by a spiritual birth. There is no substitute for the new birth. Jesus said, "Except a man be born again, he cannot see the kingdom of God."

2. *Why the new birth is necessary.* We must be born again because, as the Bible teaches, man is dead in trespasses and sins. He is dead spiritually until he is born again. Paul writes: "You hath he quickened, who were dead in trespasses and sins" (Eph. 2:1), and again, "Even when we were dead in sins, [God] hath quickened us together with Christ" (Eph. 2:5). The Bible also says that "in my flesh, dwelleth no good thing" (Rom. 7:18), and they that are in the flesh cannot please God. "That which is born of the flesh is flesh; and that which is born of the Spirit is spirit" (John 3:6).

3. *How we can experience this new birth.* John 1:12 tells us, "As many as received him [Christ], to them gave he power to become the sons of God, even to them that believe on his name." We must receive Christ—accept Him as our personal Saviour. We do so by confessing our sins and asking His forgiveness which was provided on Calvary.

Repentance from sin opens the door to forgiveness. "God . . . commandeth all men every where to repent" (Acts 17:30). "For godly sorrow worketh repentance to salvation" (2 Cor. 7:10). The words of the publican suggest this truth, "God be merciful to me a sinner" (Luke 18:13). Peter counsels the sinner, "Repent ye therefore, and be converted, that your sins may be blotted out" (Acts 3:19). And John promises, "If we confess our sins, he is faithful and just to forgive us our sins, and to cleanse us from all unrighteousness" (1 John 1:9).

Those who believe that Christ died for them, and who truly repent and receive Christ as their personal Saviour, will experience this new birth. They will be new creatures in Christ. They "shall not come into condemnation; but [are] passed from death unto life" (John 5:24).

One of the most wonderful facts about this salvation is that it is for everyone. "God is no respecter of persons" (Acts 10:34). "Whosoever shall call on the name of the Lord shall be saved" (Acts 2:21). "Come unto me, all ye that labour and are heavy laden, and I will give you rest" (Matt. 11:28). "Him that cometh to me I will in no wise cast out" (John 6:37).

There is only one way to get to heaven—that is to be saved. And we can know that we are saved—that Christ is our personal Saviour. "He that believeth on the Son of God hath the witness in himself" (1 John 5:10). "The Spirit itself beareth witness with our spirit, that we are the children of God" (Rom. 8:16).

The Bible says, "Choose you this day whom ye will serve" (Josh. 24:15). "Behold, now is the accepted time; behold now is the day of salvation" (2 Cor. 6:2). "To day if ye will hear his voice, harden not your hearts" (Heb. 3:7). "Seek ye the Lord while he may be found, call ye upon him while he is near" (Isa. 55:6). "Ye know not what shall be on the morrow" (Jas. 4:14).

The heart of the whole matter is this: "Be ye also ready: for in such an hour as ye think not the Son of man cometh" (Matt. 24:44).